THE INNER CEO

UNLEASHING LEADERS
AT ALL LEVELS

JEREMY BLAIN

Foreword by Michael Chavez, CEO Duke Corporate Education

The Inner CEO

First published in 2021 by

Panoma Press Ltd
48 St Vincent Drive, St Albans, Herts, AL1 5SJ, UK
info@panomapress.com
www.panomapress.com

Book layout by Neil Coe.

978-1-784529-33-8

DEDICATION

For Jackie, Holly and Alex.

The most supportive family I could wish for
and most certainly the leaders in our household!

PRAISE FOR THIS BOOK

I was fortunate to engage Jeremy to guide and assist me and my leadership team in transforming an organisation striving for success in an ever-changing market. It began a journey over many years that was both insightful and inspiring. Jeremy has dedicated his career to staying ahead of the game in people development and organisational design. He has an extremely broad knowledge with worldwide experience in business and organisational structure, more recently focused on the impact and opportunities that digital technology provides to innovative business leaders.

He is an inspirational and motivational individual and has an incredible wealth of operational and organisational knowledge via hands-on experience and significant research. He is very strategic in his application and has a unique ability to present solutions to challenging issues and opportunities in an easy-to-understand manner enabling successful execution.

His passion in finding solutions to build strong and successful leaders, at all levels, throughout an organisation is unending.

The Inner CEO: Unleashing leaders at all levels is a continuation of Jeremy's commitment to guiding successful and rewarding talent development.

Greg McKibbin, former regional general manager, Kodak Entertainment Imaging and Health Imaging, Asia Pacific; mentor, Small Business Mentoring Service, Australia

This is a must read for business leaders and for anyone that has ambition, desire and passion to lead. This book is so essential at a time when businesses are crying out for leadership at every level of the organisation. Read it and apply the valuable lessons that Jeremy imparts.

Paul Marks, managing director, Change Works Ltd

With the dramatically changing strategic landscape and many organisations restructuring, especially around digital, it is even more important that executive leaders embrace the opportunity for a more collective approach to leadership and business health. This allows for a more empowering approach internally and the creation of an environment where leadership at all levels can thrive. In his timely book, *The Inner CEO*, Jeremy Blain is providing organisations with the step-by-step manual to make this a reality; allowing employees at all levels to unleash their 'inner CEO', stepping up to contribute beyond their job description. *The Inner CEO* is the masterful read to show them the way.

Robin Speculand, strategy and digital implementation specialist; bestselling author

I have had three people use the term 'crisis of leadership' within the last week. The global pandemic of 2020 has shone a light on leaders like never before and the old command-and-control style of leadership has fallen apart completely for those who were too slow to recognise this before.

Good leadership has always been about equipping, empowering and allowing others to step into new roles and responsibilities as they unite around a common purpose. I am fortunate to be the

CEO of a company full of amazing people, who all participate in leading us forward, although this hasn't always been the case. If Jeremy Blain's excellent book had been around years ago, it would have helped our journey enormously, particularly in helping avoid some of my many mistakes along the way. Jeremy has long been well ahead of the curve in transforming businesses to be led by everyone, not just its leaders, and if ever there was a time to accelerate that process, it is now. If you want to be in a growing dynamic business in the 2020s, then read this book.

Paul Hargreaves, CEO, Cotswold Fayre, UK; author of *Forces for Good: Creating a better world through purpose-driven businesses*

In *The Inner CEO: Unleashing leaders at all levels*, Jeremy has captured something significant, relevant and timeless. Leadership is no longer a job title; it is no longer just action and example: it is anticipation, action and example at all levels. Jeremy goes beyond the typical mantra of employee engagement and demonstrates through case studies and interviews just how the law of stepping up applies; how thinking and behaving like a CEO is a key component for everyone in the organisation if you desire progress, whether in a startup or a scale-up.

Bob Hayward, managing partner, Be More Effective; co-author of *The Profit Secret*

As an HR practitioner, I read books about business and always think, "How do I adapt these ideas for my workplace?" Usually I am left to do the hard work myself, but not here. In *The Inner CEO*, Jeremy Blain presents a valuable blend of ideas – part thought-leadership and part practical manual – combined with intelligent suggestions, tools and activities that make it relevant to today's changing world of business. The end result is something that I will come back to time and time again.

Helen Claridge, senior HR business partner, Element Six (part of the De Beers Group)

In today's highly disruptive and digital-driven era of the fourth industrial revolution (better known as Industry 4.0), organisations need to empower not only their managerial leadership teams but also individual contributors at all levels and functional roles in enabling them to contribute towards the sustainability of the organisation in the ever-changing world of work. In *The Inner CEO*, Jeremy Blain presents a beautifully crafted guide through the process of self-leadership development with refreshingly different, and thoroughly practical, tools and frameworks to achieve this.

The book weaves in each chapter a brief introduction of key concepts, engaging interviews with business experts and industry leaders, and seemingly simple exercises, which act as a blueprint for those stepping up to unleash their inner CEO. I highly recommend this book.

Professor Sattar Bawany, CEO, The Disruptive Leadership Institute; author of *Leadership in Disruptive Times* (Business Expert Press, 2020)

In the most effective organisations great leadership can be seen everywhere, not just from the CEO or executive committee.

Individuals understand that they have not only the freedom and autonomy to lead but a responsibility to do so. Jeremy Blain's powerful book explains how to build a high-performance leadership culture and enable individuals to unleash their inner CEO. In this uncertain and fast-moving era, if there was ever a time to embrace this thinking, it is now.

Lloyd Wigglesworth, partner, The Alexander Partnership; former managing director of WHSmith News, Entertainment UK, St Ives Group, EMAP and Frontline

---

I completely agree with Jeremy Blain's central drive to unleash inner CEOs. Command-and-control management is dead. We've gone virtual and the increasingly blended combination of permanent employees and independent workers means that the workforce is now dotted across the map. It's time to increase autonomy and unleash leadership at all levels. This point is very well argued and reinforced in Blain's interview with Johanna Bolin Tingvall, global head of learning and development at Spotify. This book has come at the perfect time and it is packed with practical tips.

Richard Davies, managing director, GPS Goaltrak

Jeremy Blain's book is very well thought through and structured, with good actionable advice. No one is left behind, as the focus is on unleashing leadership at all levels.

The book not only gives guidance on the why and the what, but provides the how in the shape of models, techniques, templates and assessments; leaving no excuse for anyone to get to action. I look forward to putting my own learnings into practise, especially using some of the new tools like the Five-Point Validation star.

I'd recommend all human capital and HR leaders to read *The Inner CEO* to help shape their organisations for today's workplace challenges and needs.

Jennifer Gillespie, HR director (South East Asia), Xylem

In today's world of exponential change and uncertain future, *The Inner CEO* is extremely relevant and action-orientated. It shows clearly how change can be accelerated by unleashing leadership skills in each and everyone in the organisation. By following the suggestions and actions in this extremely timely book, organisations can create a deeper purpose, allowing people to be creative and empowered by going beyond their job description. Finally, this is a book that outlines why this is important, what needs to happen and the all-important how to get it done.

I have known Jeremy for about 10 years, including his time in Singapore, when he was CEO, Asia Pacific, for an international training company. I have admired his journey, his research, his passion, his knowledge and his desire to support leaders around the world to successfully transform their businesses and workforces. *The Inner CEO* takes Jeremy's journey one step forward and recognises that we have entered a new age of empowerment. This book is the blueprint to make it a reality in organisations everywhere.

Sunil Narang, president and CEO, WDHB Inc, Denver, CO, USA

I have worked with and for companies, where only the top levels of executive leadership were referred to as 'leaders'. This has immense negative consequences for the culture, leading to a poor leadership culture on all levels. It results in transactional people management, since you can't whip out your ability to inspire, empower and ensure that your team's talent is fully unleashed from one day to the next.

Jeremy Blain's book, *The Inner CEO*, provides a highly efficient and practical road map for such companies to empower their teams and 'supercharge growth'. In the book's own words, "It's not only about supercharging your employees' growth – your company will grow alongside your team when they are empowered to perform."

Especially in today's fast-moving and highly competitive environment, we must embrace the notion that everyone – regardless of experience, title, salary and number of direct reports – can inspire others to follow them and act on their ideas. That is what leadership is: when you can inspire others to follow the ideas that you are enthusiastically and competently presenting, you're a leader.

The Inner CEO, by Jeremy Blain, thanks to its wide appeal, practical approach and skilfully curated advice is a deeply insightful, must-read for those interested in making their organisation more successful through the empowerment of their entire workforce. In addition, it is written in easy language and with interviews that make it a highly entertaining business read.

Mette Johansson, founder and owner, MetaMind Training; founder and chair, KeyNote Women Speakers; co-founder, Inclusive Leaders Institute

Like Jeremy Blain, I am passionate about the benefits of digitalisation and transforming businesses for the future. Especially around the future of work. Which is why I co-founded YourFLOCK.co.uk. But also like Jeremy, I know this is not just about the technology stack you have.

The future of work is all about the very soul of our organisations. It's about human values and how people work together. To succeed in the modern workplace organisations need to adapt, challenge traditional structures and unlock the power within the changing workforce. That is done by a culture shift that underpins a new age of empowerment. This is why *The Inner CEO* is the book for now.

We have all talked about 'leadership at all levels' but nothing really exists as a how-to guide for both the business leadership and the employees themselves. *The Inner CEO* provides the rationale and the blueprint to make it happen for real. With a more collective approach to organisational leadership, that encourages everyone to step up and go beyond their job description.

Jeremy Blain's book is full of examples, interviews, new models, tools and even a complete 90-Day Road Map to accelerate such action. It's practical, well researched and will help many organisations as they embrace the age of empowerment and unleash leaders at all levels. This combined with a more values driven approach to working together especially remotely – empowered by new technologies like YourFLOCK – will be one of the ingredients to the secret sauce for business success in the post-covid world.

Dan Sodergren, co-founder, YourFlock.co.uk; head of diversity, Manchester Publicity Association; founder, Great Marketing Works; technology futurist and advocate, BBC TV and News, BBC Radio

With *The Inner CEO*, Jeremy Blain touches on the core of organisational success. His actionable research around developing sustainable leadership and creating an acute sense of personal empowerment is transformational. Jeremy provides critical insights and valuable tips from industry leaders and business experts to successfully prepare us for a new empowered future of work. An inspirational and transformative read.

Jerome Barthe, group HR talent director, International SOS

Jeremy Blain's book, *The Inner CEO*, echoes very much what I have always believed in: that we all have powers within us, waiting to be discovered, developed, maximised and shared.

Jeremy strongly captures the why, what and how to unleash the inner CEO. As he wrote, the concept is both mindset and action. "It is about leadership belief, and about taking ownership to make something happen; often beyond a job role and outside traditional KPIs."

The interviews with business experts and industry leaders, together with the 90-Day Road Map and other toolkits and templates, make the concepts very applicable and tangible. Those implementing Jeremy's recommendations in their organisations will undoubtedly see the rewards and fruits of their investments.

Elaine Bernalyn S Cercado, managing director and executive coach, POWERinU Training and Coaching LLP

Blain is addressing a critical need to engage the workforce, at all levels, in his book, *The Inner CEO.*

For two and a half decades, I have supported and partnered with leaders who are driving change. Over this period, we have researched times of transformation. We often asked, "What will create the tipping point?" We speculated that it might be the convergence of emerging technologies, global connectedness, demographic shifts, and changing employee and consumer behaviour. We knew that the advent of a pandemic was real, but truly did not take this into real consideration. But here we are. Blain provides a practical path to engaging the workforce, in every capacity, to think and act like an 'In-Role CEO'. We often refer to the importance of engagement, but this explosively fast business transformation requires much more than engagement. We need to unleash our inner CEOs in every capacity, at every level; Blain's book provides the road map and how-to for getting it done.

Laura Goodrich, one of The 10 Most Inspiring Businesswomen to Watch, 2020 USA; co-founder, GWT Next; bestselling author of *Seeing Red Cars: Driving Yourself, Your Team and Your Organization to a Positive Future*

Jeremy and I have shared stages, screens and panel discussions and I have always witnessed him 'walking the walk' as an executive leader. He practises what he preaches, and I know his teams have always felt empowered to lead at their level. It is no wonder that accelerated success of the businesses he led and managed, while fuelling high degrees of loyalty between him and his team. There was no how-to manual; no road map to make it happen; it was self-learned and self-taught.

I am delighted, therefore, to support Jeremy's launch of his new book *The Inner CEO*. This provides readers at senior organisational levels *and* individual contributors with the blueprint to usher in a brand new age of empowerment. The book establishes early on what this means, why it is important and then spends quality time getting into the 'how-to' detail. It is a book that will make it a reality for those wanting to step up beyond their job description, and for those executive leaders who are ready to truly sponsor leadership at all levels in their organisations.

There is no better timing for a book like this, and the accompanying interviews with business, human capital and learning leaders bring the concept alive in a way that makes it so practical and so of the 'now'.

Buy it, read it and implement it now!

Dr Tanvi Gautam, CEO Leadershift Inc., multi-award winning keynote speaker, author and executive coach

---

At the core of every single one of us lies the desire to be seen and heard for who we are and who we have the potential to be. True to his character and everything that he represents, Jeremy has successfully created a practical and inspirational guide to help individuals at all levels of their career discover their inner CEO, step up, and be seen for the talent they truly are. I highly recommend this book for anyone ready to level up and any organisation ready to transform itself from the inside out.

Carlii Lyon, personal branding coach and founder of The Brand in You

---

In today's uncertainty, success will come to those who embrace their inner CEO and a culture of experimentation, boldness and trust. Jeremy Blain's practical tools and pragmatic insights are road tested in leading organisations. Use them to invite your inner CEO to thrive.

Joanne Flinn, author of *Karma: How To Stay Calm and Productive through Coronavirus to the Recovery*. Former country head financial services consulting, PwC

ACKNOWLEDGEMENTS

There are so many people who have been a part of this journey. If I remember correctly, I launched the idea (and commitment to actually do it!) at an industry event in 2017. Four years later, it's incredible to see it in print and as a digital book.

First off, a massive thanks to one-time customer, colleague, friend and now mentor, Greg McKibbin. Over dozens of catch-ups across Singapore and Melbourne, Greg helped me thrash out the concept and, in true Aussie style, did not let me get away with waffle, ill-considered ideas or doubt when hitting roadblocks. His belief, as a global leader, in the subject matter and his support of my vision have been greatly appreciated.

Huge thanks also to a trio of book coaches who supported me through the process. First and foremost is Rachel Henke, whom I'd recommend to anyone thinking about getting their first business book from idea to reality. She has been the engine behind the journey. Alongside Rachel was Russell Cooper, whose advice around flow, sense and messaging were always on the money.

At the latter stages, as we got into deeper proofreading, design, formatting and the final version, I'd like to thank Rebecca Duffy who took the manuscript by the scruff of the neck and helped get it into its designed, formatted and publishable shape. In parallel I'd like to thank long-time collaborator Mohamed Khalid Maideen for excellent design work, bringing to life the models in the book and the front cover, which I feel strongly conveys the spirit behind the subject matter.

There were six people closely involved as the glue between the chapters in my book. They were my expert interviewees, whose passion for the subject matter, and practical action in their own businesses to make leadership at all levels actually happen, has provided readers with workable ideas, must-dos, 'watch outs' and best practices. Big thanks to Johanna Bolin Tingvall, Spotify; Philippe Bonnet, Essilor; Steen Puggaard, co-founder of the phenomenal 4Fingers Crispy Chicken; Natasha Prasad, Mambu; Emma Saxby, talent, HR expert and coach; and the wonderful Andrea Studlik, JLL. Thanks too, to Tilo Sequeira, also at Spotify, for her encouragement along the way.

Thanks to all those who have been sounding boards for the idea and journey over the last three years, primarily my previous team in Singapore who were there from the very beginning – Belinda Ng, Antonio Codinach, Minh Thuy Phi, Rosalind Loh and Sandy Hernandez. Respect to you lot!

A big shout out to Theresa Cheng, Don Rapley, Prof Sattar Bawany and his great family Nora, Danial and Adam; Elaine, Elijah and Dick Cercado; Amita, Manish, Nia and Aniya Chawda (our good mates in Singapore); Tanvi Gautam (who would have dragged me kicking and screaming to complete this book had I not made progress!), Jennifer Gillespie, Nigel Signal, Dr Rochelle Haynes, Robin Speculand, Dr Michael Netzley, Tara Treanor, Ken Govan, Anne Boisier-Fouché, Yasuhiro Minatoya, Richard Davies, Paul Marks, Akira Furumoto, Mr Global Nomad himself – Kevin Cottam – and many more. Last but not least, a big thanks to Steve Ashcroft: my first ever line manager when I joined Procter & Gamble in 1990. Even then, Steve epitomised the very spirit of this book. He empowered, supported and inspired those who worked with and for him. I have always appreciated that and kept in touch. I'm now thankful to count Steve as one of my good friends.

My sincerest apologies to anyone I have inadvertently missed off. So many have been there for me and I thank you for it.

Finally, a big thank you to my mum, dad and brother – Carolyn, Raymond and Richard Blain – for all their support. I finally did it!

FOREWORD BY **MICHAEL CHAVEZ**

Michael Chavez is CEO of Duke Corporate Education.

With Sudanshu Palsule, Michael is co-author of *Rehumanizing Leadership: Putting Purpose Back into Business.*

Back in the 1990s, after graduating from business school, I landed my first job at a boutique strategy consulting firm, which turned out to be a crucible of learning about strategic thinking, collaboration and analytical rigour. After successive roles in strategic planning at two different Fortune 500 companies, I started to realise that despite the cognitive stimulation that came with my work, the best conversations seemed to happen after I left the room. There was something going on – let's call it 'leadership' – that seemed to determine whether or not the strategies my team and I had recommended would work or even move forward toward an execution plan.

After nearly 20 years in the learning and leadership development space, I've become ever more curious about not only how leadership happens, but where, and in what circumstances, especially when it comes to aligning whole organisations.

The Inner CEO positions leadership – operational and strategic – as something that can be owned by anyone, regardless of level, function, experience or role. Thus it is relevant to many. It is for executive leaders, offering inspiration as to how they can create an organisational culture of experimentation, boldness and trust. It is aimed at HR professionals and line managers, guiding them through this culture change with practical, innovative professional development strategies. And it is for individual contributors at all levels, providing the tools to help them to unleash their inner CEO and become an 'in-role CEO': empowered to lead with creativity, innovation and purpose.

Why is such a transformation urgent and necessary now? For perspective, I work for one of the top leadership education firms in the world. This has allowed me to build a career on developing the mid to upper levels of leadership of some of the world's leading businesses across six continents. It has also afforded me the opportunity to talk frequently to the bosses of those leaders. In these C-suite conversations, I normally pose a question or two about their biggest worry regarding leadership in their organisations. Almost universally, especially over the past 10 years, I've heard some version of the following response:

> What my team and I need from these leaders is more participation, push-back, involvement and co-creating of our strategy. We're simply too far from the action; things are moving too fast and the situation is too complex to expect strategy to be a one-way cascade. Moreover, we don't know much about digital transformation. We simply can't do it alone. We don't have the time to wait for them to feel asked. We need them to jump in, even if it's uncomfortable.

This worry, along with an environment of accelerating complexity, disruption and pace is, I worked out, a driver behind why 'courage' has become so fashionable in leadership circles today.

I've even been asked to try to 'teach' courage, which is, of course, as ridiculous as it sounds. But on the other hand, I find it helpful to think of four critical conditions as being necessary in order for an act to be 'courageous' (I reference the work of Cliff Bolster from Case Western University).

For an act to be courageous, the person undertaking it must:

1. Sense fear or anxiety associated with the action.

2. Genuinely believe that the action will result in negative consequences for them, based upon a rational assessment of the situation.

3. Have the perception of a free choice.

Allow me to pause. So far, this represents an act of carelessness. So, what makes it courageous? The fourth condition, which is that the person undertaking this action must also:

4. Be in pursuit of a supraordinate goal. This last one means that the action must also involve taking a stand for something bigger than oneself.

In *Rehumanizing Leadership: Putting Purpose Back into Business*, my co-author and I explore the importance of purpose, empathy and meaning, not just at an organisational level, but also at a team and individual level, in creating the conditions for alignment, success and sustainability. We found that not only are purpose, values and vision fast becoming the key levers for building clarity and focusing organisational energy broadly, but also that they provide the guardrails necessary to help individuals step up to leadership in the moments of truth that call for it.

We live in an age where everyone must live and breathe purpose-based leadership if organisations are to exhibit the agility needed to survive. The good news is that we are finally admitting to ourselves, after all the how-to books on the complex task of leadership have been written, that tapping into our underlying humanity – our empathy, values, sense of purpose and desire to contribute to the betterment of other humans – is the best formula for leadership. And it has been under our noses the whole time. Furthermore, we're realising that this is a *shared* experience. All must feel and act from their own humanity, and this, it turns out, is leadership.

Executive leaders need courage to truly unleash leadership at all levels: they must let go of the day to day and trust their people to lead without having to ask for permission. This book calls on middle and senior-level leaders to support a new age of empowerment in their organisations and it shows how teams can take ownership and experiment, through coaching and through a human-centred leadership approach. *The Inner CEO* will arm leaders and managers with the know-how to make this a reality in their organisation, as well as guiding individuals who are ready to step up as unleashed 'in-role CEOs'.

Far beyond a democratic movement which is about how power is distributed, shared leadership is about how *clarity* is distributed. Jeremy Blain's invitation to unleash our inner CEOs is no less than a rethink of how we can transform organisations into powerhouses of leadership at all levels. This, I believe, will lead to more productive, sustainable and thriving institutions. Ultimately, it is an exploration of how we can step up without waiting to be asked. It is an invitation to jump in and try it out. Yes, it takes courage, but if that courage is based on your humanity, it will not only be worth it, but it will energise and nourish others.

I hope you accept the invitation wholeheartedly and while you're at it, 'forward' it to all.

Michael Chavez, CEO Duke Corporate Education
August 2020

Rehumanizing Leadership: Putting Purpose Back into Business
by Michael Chavez and Sudanshu Palsule is available at
rehumanizingleadership.com

PREFACE

We are entering a new age of empowerment. Leadership at all levels can become the reality many have been striving for. We must unleash the inner CEO within our people and create the conditions where everyone has the opportunity to contribute beyond their job role, more strategically across the broader organisation.

In this groundbreaking book, author and business transformation expert Jeremy Blain sets out exactly how to achieve this reality. Unleashing leadership at all levels and creating in-role CEOs drives a more collective and collaborative approach to organisational growth, while releasing executive leaders, non-executive directors and boards to focus on navigating an increasingly uncertain future.

There are many books on leadership, management, soft skills and business in general, but very few which focus on leadership at all levels. Jeremy Blain has corrected this anomaly and provides an action-oriented, how-to manual for organisations, leaders and those ready to unleash their inner CEO to contribute beyond their job description.

The Inner CEO: Unleashing leaders at all levels will arm leaders with the steps to make this a reality in their organisation, as well as individuals who are ready to step up as unleashed in-role CEOs.

The book lays out the required conditions at organisational and executive leadership level to set this up for success, and not doom it to failure before it starts. *The Inner CEO* then provides a 90-Day Road Map, assessment tool, skills profiling and Personal Development Mosaic; and an action toolkit to provide you with everything you need for successful implementation.

Throughout the book there are featured interviews with business, HR, and global learning leaders, sharing how their organisations have created the conditions for leadership at all levels to flourish, including what it takes to make it happen successfully, and the many traps to avoid. The organisations featured include global multinationals, startups, a fintech business and the new-breed, high-growth technology and lifestyle company, Spotify.

At the end of the book, you will have the rationale, the conditions required for success, an organisation-level action plan, and individual next steps for those stepping up to unleash their inner CEO. Read on…

CONTENTS

INTRODUCTION

From the early days of my career, I have always attempted to step up and go beyond my job roles. I noticed that in some organisations, it was easy to do, whereas in others, I was constrained by a traditional management structure that did not encourage or even acknowledge the benefits of truly empowering people. As I progressed through my career, this empowerment was often referred to as 'leadership at any level'.

I call it 'unleashing the inner CEO'. In other words, empowering individual contributors – regardless of level, function, experience or role – to contribute to the wider business, operationally and strategically. The concept of unleashing the inner CEO encapsulates both mindset and action. It is about leadership belief, and about taking ownership to make something happen; often beyond a job role and outside traditional key performance indicators (KPIs). The jobs in which I was supported to unleash my inner CEO were those where I was encouraged to think and contribute strategically outside my core job role while managing my performance at an operational level. This was a win-win for the business and for me.

As I evolved into a business leader, learning professional and human resources expert, I began to empower and train people to unleash *their* inner CEO. I did this not only with our permanent employees but also with an increasingly independent workforce of highly valued collaborators, resulting in more significant mutual benefit, appreciation and loyalty. These can be hard to come by in our fast-changing times.

I encouraged this form of leadership at all levels across my increasingly blended workforce (permanent and independent workers; office-based and remote) in my own way, with help from experts I respected, without necessarily having a how-to manual.

That helped me more rapidly create in-role CEOs: individual contributors whose leadership and strategic potential is developed and activated regardless of their official job description. This is the embodiment of the unleashed inner CEO.

There are huge opportunities over the next decade and beyond: a think-differently mindset and transformation have been fast-tracked by reactions to the pandemic of coronavirus disease (Covid-19). At the same time, the execution and implementation of new and vital supporting structures – such as new rules of the road, the mobilisation of remote workers, learning support, evolved human resources frameworks, in-role coaching and more – continue to present considerable challenges. If we've learned anything from the global financial crisis, geopolitical turmoil and uncertainty around the world including the more recent US-China trade issues, as well as the Covid-19 pandemic, it's that organisations must rapidly transform and continually adapt to the times.

Many are crying out for a new business model to help them successfully transform at digital and human levels and propel their organisations into a prosperous and exciting future. Such a model must drive more collective and collaborative leadership through unleashing the power of people, and will be enabled by appropriate technologies, flatter structures and repurposed line management. This book provides the toolkit for this transformation.

My goal in this book is to guide you on an exciting journey into the possibilities in the emerging world of work, where you will discover what we can do in the face of continuing, radical transformation. At the heart of successful change is a new approach to strategic and operational leadership. Unleashing the inner CEOs in our organisations is no longer a choice: it's a must-do. This is especially the case if we are to build a more collective, engaged approach to strategy implementation and ownership of critical actions. This approach benefits our business, employees, customers and other stakeholders.

Before writing *The Inner CEO*, I evaluated the market and realised that there was a multitude of books on leadership (focused on executive leaders, management and soft skills). I could not, however, find any textbooks or specifically designed training for employees at all levels to help them develop leadership skills in their existing roles. I found no manuals, personal development plans or best practice guides – apart from a few case studies – that existed to help people step up, develop and drive their leadership capability forward, regardless of their level in the organisation.

So, this book is stepping into that space, and addresses the audiences for whom this transformation is most relevant. Whether you're a board member, non-executive director, CEO, human resources professional, learning and development expert, line manager, employee or independent worker, this is the perfect book for you. It will help you realise the power inside you and within your people, unleashing inner CEOs and encouraging leadership at all levels in the organisation. A more agile, collective, collaborative and modern approach for uncertain, dispersed times.

As you read the book, you will be armed with precise implementation steps, including a 90-Day Road Map, an assessment tool, skills profiling and an action toolkit to give you everything you need for success. This means that you will start in the right way and build momentum as you measure results from day one, which will be a crucial foundation for the journey. This is a journey that must be successful. Too much is at stake for our organisations and our people, as we look ahead to the next 10 years and beyond.

- Chapter 1, Welcome to the Fourth Industrial Revolution, provides context, outlining where we stand now and identifying five vectors of transformation (The Five Forces).

- Chapter 2, A New Approach for Changing Times, presents the essentials of what is meant by the inner CEO, and the four elements of the unleashed inner CEO: Envision, Engage, Execute and Excel.

- Chapter 3, Creating the Right Conditions to Unleash In-Role CEOs, provides guidance, especially relevant for leaders, on how to create the right culture and mindset for empowerment across the organisation.

- Chapter 4, Supercharging Organisational Progress, guides leaders, human resources (HR) professionals and managers as to how they can drive this culture change at an operational level.

- Chapter 5, Making it Happen: Unleashing Leadership at All Levels, covers the steps to be taken towards unleashing the inner CEO. It presents a practical, accessible programme that will enable individuals to embark on this journey, with the support of managers, HR professionals and their colleagues.

- Chapter 6, Measuring Employee Empowerment, sets out an empowering approach to measurement. It provides the means for individuals, managers and leaders to track the impact of unleashing the inner CEO, on themselves, on their teams, and on the organisation as a whole.

- Finally, Chapter 7, The Opportunity to Reimagine Our Organisations, looks ahead to the challenges and choices of the 21st century, a call to action to organisations to incorporate the models and learning in this book.

It's worth noting that, throughout, I use the word 'talent' as distinct from 'Talent'. Without a capital letter, 'talent' includes not only everyone in an organisation, but also the wider devolved workforce of independent workers and digital nomads, and the prospective talent of the future. Talent with a capital 'T' has been exclusive and applied to the chosen few. In this book, talent is inclusive and provides an opportunity for everyone.

In parallel with creating the framework and training content for this book, I decided to bring the concept alive by exploring existing best practices and expertise, and so the book is full of practical advice, models and actionable steps. I interviewed a variety of business experts and industry leaders: CEOs, talent and human capital professionals, as well as learning leaders from a broad range of businesses including Spotify, Essilor, 4Fingers Crispy Chicken, JLL and more. In these interviews, they share their experiences and unique perspectives on the value of unleashing inner CEOs at all levels, and in different businesses. They highlight the ingredients for success while underpinning the rapid cultural shifts required to make progress. The interviews complement each of the chapters and are sprinkled throughout.

The Inner CEO fills a gaping hole in the market, and I believe this is the perfect time to unleash the reality of considered and strongly supported leadership-at-all-levels in our organisations, globally. In essence, this book is the how-to manual for creating in-role CEOs who go beyond the day to day and start to contribute more strategically to the broader business.

In this book, I give you *the* way to accelerate transformation, unleash the power of your people and supercharge growth. At a time when many businesses are struggling to survive in such a challenging and unpredictable environment, let alone evolve for future success, you will get access to the tools, techniques and skills to succeed.

Let's begin.

CHAPTER 1:

Welcome to the Fourth Industrial Revolution

Introduction

Industry 4.0, the Fourth Industrial Revolution, or the digital era, represents the coming together of the physical, the biological and the technological for the first time in human history. The velocity and systems impact of this revolution make it distinct from industrial revolutions of the past. It is quite a moment, and I truly believe we can be inspired by the possibilities it presents for those willing to embrace it.

Many people still visualise the term 'Industrial Revolution' as a black and white image of a winding gear turning above coal mines, with choking smoke billowing from towering chimney stacks, and a labour force crammed on to factory floors. Few relics remain from the now-declined industrial revolutions of the past: rusting wheels, abandoned chimneys, and derelict, coal dust-covered factories.

Each industrial revolution has caused widespread, heavy casualties for businesses that do not respond to their changing environment. Corporations that are unable, or unwilling, to adapt to the wave of innovation coming their way are marked for certain failure. Revolutions by definition bring change, and each of the four main industrial revolutions – the 1784 water and steam mechanical revolution; the 1870 mass production and electrical energy revolution; the third revolution of 1969 with the introduction of IT and electronics, and today, the fourth revolution of cyber-physical systems: the digital age – has changed the world.

We've witnessed a stream of well-known brands becoming casualties when management teams failed to adapt. Gary Vaynerchuk said of Kodak and Toys R Us, "They did not innovate, and when you do not innovate you die."[1]

Today, we are in a unique position: the Fourth Industrial Revolution – Industry 4.0 – is upon us. Leaders must adjust, realign and build a new mentality and approach to leadership in their organisations. A call to action is necessary to unleash the potential of our leaders at all levels in an organisation. This is the opportunity we must grasp, in order to engage with the forces of transformation. This chapter sets out the context of these forces, and is therefore imperative for executive leaders, managers and individual contributors to understand.

The Five Forces of Transformation

The fast pace of how we live and work today is driving incremental and radical change in business and is becoming the new normal. Some organisations are coping with this fast-paced change, but many are being left behind. The rate of change is catching companies unaware, across the globe. Transforming organisations to prepare them for the future is no longer a question of when and whether it's a good idea; it has become an urgent question of how to transform.

In the current workplace and beyond, we will experience dramatic shifts as we encounter a perfect storm of forces that will challenge our companies, leaders, managers and teams on a worldwide scale. These five forces will serve to either propel or block the success of businesses in this transformational era.

Figure 1: The Five Forces of Transformation

The organisations which embrace and drive the agenda in these areas do so because they have understood how central each force is to attaining competitive advantage now, as well as to protecting their customers' experience in the future. This is why I frequently explain to my clients that the future of work is now. There is no time for the luxury of delay.

Organisations which don't take action now won't be prepared to weather the storm that is the Fourth Industrial Revolution.

At the centre of this new revolution is a digital threat that determines whether a company maintains its competitive advantage or whether it is left in the dust of the old era. For this reason, it's critical for leaders to shift their thinking now, which will inform how to reshape the organisation's culture, and enable a move into the what and the how of implementation.

The key to success is blending the human touch with the new technologies. To achieve this, the culture of our workplaces must be ready to truly challenge and empower every member of the organisation to unleash their inner CEO.

Force One: Digital Transformation

The first force is digital. A digital transformation is necessary to harness the power of Industry 4.0, the digital revolution. A mentality shift is essential, at leadership level and throughout the organisation, to facilitate this change. The most successful organisations are making strides and undergoing a fundamental change, whereas others who are unwilling to change are already falling behind.

There are various elements that we must bear in mind when we talk about the digital force. It's vital to look at what's going to happen in the next 10 years. This is a critical period in preparing to succeed in the digital era.

The advent of artificial intelligence (AI) and robotics is pivotal. AI will be everywhere; it will be used by everyone and be in everything that we use. This is from a lifestyle point of view as well as a business perspective. AI will become more intelligent and efficient because the technology that is unleashing the capability of true artificial intelligence is 5G (fifth-generation wireless technology) and quantum computing, which will be more and more widely available. 5G is underestimated by many organisations because they don't understand that it is more than just faster internet. It's not designed to be a solution for implementing outdated systems faster: it is a new system in itself. It is *the* future enabler to move the business forward.

5G is the immediate gamechanger that will make the digital era possible. It's about 10 times as fast as 4G, and about twice as fast as your standard broadband. This is the technology that can run smart cities and autonomous vehicles, and can translate huge racks of data in seconds. But when I talk to people, they say things like, "Oh yes, we can put more video on our website." Many business leaders don't understand the potential of 5G. Faster video is merely scratching the surface.

5G will inherently shift things to the cloud. That's why Microsoft, as you may already know, moved from being a computing company to a cloud company, as did Amazon, moving away from digitally enabled retail. The Amazon cloud is one of the most used systems of its kind out there for large organisations, particularly for those changing their business model so that it is ready for the new digital era.

While 5G is the immediate gamechanger, all eyes will be on the quantum computing breakthrough, as we move from the theoretical space into reality in the 2020s. According to Stephen Shankland, writing in CNET.com,[2] quantum computing was given a boost in 2019 when Google declared 'quantum supremacy' – a step towards making quantum computers a reality. With increasing speed and power available to researchers over the next five years, commentators expect to see tangible progress and results from those leading the field (including Google, IBM, Rigetti Computing, Amazon, Microsoft, China with it Micius satellite technology and others). In 2018, Amit Katwala[3] reported in wired.co.uk that quantum computing had become the most significant focus for technological supremacy in the Chinese government. This ambition is certainly matched by its cash investments.

The Chinese government has made quantum science the focus of a 'megaproject' and set its sights on breakthroughs in quantum communications and quantum computing. It is reportedly investing $10bn in building the National Laboratory for Quantum Information Sciences in Hefei.

Technologies such as 5G, quantum and micro-combs[4] will release the potential of concepts such as smart cities, immersive gaming, autonomous vehicles and the Internet of Things. Simply put, every device, every app and every system will be connected, rather than accessed individually: a connected ecosystem for a truly connected life. Added to this, technology that we can wear ('wearables') and innovations we will soon be able to integrate into our bodies (such as smart blood, health indicators, wellness monitors and more) will mean that everything can be connected, accessed and utilised through one tool. Most likely, this will be driven and managed by more intelligent and intuitive AI, powered by tech such as 5G, micro-combs and quantum: the gamechangers.

To prepare the way for this fundamental shift, organisations that are currently locked into legacy systems, processes and products will need to shift into a mentality of ecosystems. This will require the use of platforms such as apps to connect everything, so they can provide an enhanced customer experience. This means also linking their systems with customer systems. To do so, they will have to be on board with understanding technology and data, data protection and cyber risk: significant challenges for many.

Most organisations, as you may imagine, aren't ready to tackle this monumental shift. It has been predicted that by the mid-2020s, cyber risk could cost $7 trillion worldwide, making it equivalent to a top-10 world economy. Therefore, the companies grasping what going digital means, from a technology point of view, will have a competitive advantage. This understanding is a crucial feature of the digital force.

It's a dramatic mentality shift, and it has to happen at the leadership and management levels. From my research, I found a lack of understanding to be the biggest block to progress in this area. Almost half of all leaders surveyed did not have a vision for the digital era; and 40% of those had no intention of developing one.[5]

Force Two: Leadership Readiness (or 'The Emperor's New Clothes')

The second force is about leadership readiness – what I call the emperor's new clothes. Many leaders and managers in traditional businesses talk a good game, but do not have the capability to define and implement the necessary strategies and actions required for robust business transformation. And by that, I mean both digital and human transformation.

As workforces become more dispersed and remote, leaders need people to take ownership of their roles in a way that most have never done before. For better customer experience, organisations will need to encourage higher levels of collaboration in their teams. This is why, in this new digital environment, it is possible to give everyone, at every level, the opportunity to unleash their inner CEO. If you have the right digital thread in place, it can facilitate this type of empowerment, so that people can truly take ownership of their contribution. Leaders need to lead this evolution and managers will need to understand how to manage differently and through new, enabling digital technologies.

In my research for a digital white paper, *Transforming Your Company into a Digital-Driven Business*, published in February 2019 and updated in May 2020, I found that 40% of leaders across three continents[6] – America, Asia and Europe – were not ready for a business model transformation and had no digital vision for their organisation. Furthermore, 40% of them were not committed to adopting a vision, which translated into almost half of the companies not being ready. What this means is that nearly half the companies we studied in this survey were setting themselves up to fail, not to succeed. This is a crisis at the leadership level and must be tackled, so that organisations are in a better position to future-proof themselves and to prosper. To tackle this, we need to ask what can be done from the bottom up, rather than from the top down. Top-down approaches don't seem to be working as they once did, so it makes sense to deal with the crisis differently. If leaders aren't willing to change, how can an organisation truly transform, and how can people be empowered to take ownership? We need to unlock and unleash our CEOs at all levels, not constrain them.

Two things appear to be happening here. On one hand, there is an attitude issue (40% of leaders not considering adopting a digital vision) and a skill issue. Some leaders 'don't know what they don't know' and are immobilised, genuinely not knowing what to do, how to do it or when. It seems that we need an extraordinary event to force the issue; this was presented by the recent pandemic and the move to immediate, digitalised, remote working. It was no accident that Covid-19 became the second biggest accelerator of digital transformation and leadership buy-in since the smartphone was launched in 2007. It forced the issue and took choice away. 'Need to do' was finally on everyone's lips.

This is where the mentality shift needs to move from a *discussion* of what digital means, to an *understanding* of what it is, and *how to execute and implement it,* so the organisation can thrive in the new 4.0 business era. Otherwise, these ill-prepared leaders may sound good, but their companies will fail due to lack of understanding, appropriate action and thought-through engagement of the rest of the business.

According to Forbes[7] and IBM,[8] 84% of digital transformations have failed at the execution stage. Bridges Business Consultancy said that traditional strategy fails about 60% to 63% of the time.[9] These figures are a telling indication of the scale of the challenge inherent in digital transformations, and the importance of genuine leadership readiness.

Force Three: Organisational Culture Shift

These forces build one upon the other, and as you are undoubtedly beginning to see, the cultural shift is possible only when leaders understand the scope of digital 4.0. When the leadership team is committed and ready, it creates the mentality for thinking about questions such as, "What are the values and behaviours that will underpin our culture change, so that we all thrive in this new era?"

A definition of a thriving culture for the digital era is that it is adaptable and responsive to the vast opportunities, as well as the formidable threats and challenges, presented by technology, the disruption of markets, changing customer behaviours, the evolving workforce mix and changing ways of working. Ultimately it is the blend of the digital and the human touch that will be paramount to achieving the necessary cultural shift. And, as detailed in the second force, culture shift starts at the leadership level. If it isn't in place at the top, it won't happen throughout the organisation.

An inspiring example of an organisation that has successfully facilitated this shift is DBS Bank in south-east Asia. It has been repeatedly recognised by the Euromoney Awards as the best digital bank in the world. The CEO, Piyush Gupta, said, "If you want to compete, you must embrace the digital and the human touch together, and build the new culture around that."[10]

Fundamental to the bank's success was its ability to take risks and its willingness to experiment to understand what worked and what didn't, while maintaining its focus on the customer. It appears to be obsessed with continuous change and data-driven decision-making, which is paying off for the bank. Ultimately, the biggest success factors are first, to understand that you're on a technological voyage, and second, that it is a significant culture shift for your organisation. You simply cannot separate the digital from the necessary human journey. It's as one.

By engaging with the forces of digital transformation and leadership readiness, the big culture shift required for the digital era becomes possible. And by achieving the culture shift, the hierarchy is flattened, and the rest of the people in the organisation are supported and encouraged to unleash their inner CEO, which essentially means maximising their potential, whatever their current role in the organisational hierarchy. This is an excellent example of what happens when you seize the opportunity of digital transformation and leadership readiness and segue seamlessly into the third force, that of organisational culture shift.

Force Four: The Future Workforce and Ways of Working

How do we maximise human capital in this new era, and what about the future workforce? These are fascinating topics, which

I've invested years in researching and understanding. The primary consideration is the new blended or hybrid workforce. What I mean by this is the evolution of how we hire our human resource. My latest paper, *The Blended Workforce Revolution*, written in partnership with Dr Rochelle Haynes,[11] was published in February 2020, and considered this very trend.[12]

Important questions arising from our research included:

- Will we continue to hire a predominantly permanent resource?
- Will we begin to integrate independent specialist workers into our workforce?
- How will so-called digital nomads become an invaluable part of the workforce to supplement areas where technology skills are scarce?

Our workforce mix includes increasing numbers of independent workers and contractors. So how will human capital management need to evolve if it is to create a brand new framework that encompasses a broader definition of any organisation's human resources?

How will we employ AI and potentially, in some industries, robotics to work alongside humans? Particularly when new enabling technologies such as 5G and quantum computing revolutionise artificial intelligences and how they can be deployed, alongside and within our broader human capital mix.

When appraising the future workforce, the essential factor to consider is an organisation's key people, whether they're permanent or freelance, and how to give them what they need so they can take enthusiastic ownership of their role in the organisation. For example, how will more neurodiverse individuals – such as those on the autistic spectrum – be brought into appropriate jobs? Emerging job roles may require unique skill sets, such as the inherent ability to understand patterns in numbers and data, attention to specific details, mathematical and rapid scientific understanding and more (see *The Fifth Force: Broadening Diversity Lenses* below).

People must be encouraged to embrace the digital tools and new ways of working in order to take ownership of what they're doing and collaborate with their peers, seniors, subordinates, customers and partners, to an extent they never have before. There will be more remote and distributed workers or freelance digital nomads. How will they be managed so that they are supported to do something amazing in their organisation – or the organisation they are working on behalf of – whatever their role, level or location?

The Fifth Force: Broadening Diversity Lenses

All that has been traditionally evaluated in terms of diversity and inclusion is now becoming increasingly complex, due to the evolving diversity of the future workforce, as covered in *Force Four: The Future Workforce and Ways of Working*. This provides a momentous opportunity and challenge, depending on the organisation's ability to harness the power of these forces. This incredible transformation of the future workforce requires a broadening of traditional diversity lenses, and with it, increased tolerance and inclusion. This should be done in a manner that unleashes people's inner CEO and drives a sense of leadership throughout the entire organisation.

Conversely, unleashing leadership at all levels means to challenge interpretations of leadership and reinterpret it with a broader diversity lens. For example, at the time of writing, only 37 Fortune 500 companies were led by a female CEO: an all-time high.[13] In July 2020, the Colour of Power survey[14] found that only 51 of the top 1,100 most powerful jobs in the UK (4.7%) were occupied by non-white individuals, at a point when black, Asian and minority ethnic people represented 13% of the population. Alongside the moral case, reinforced strongly by the Black Lives Matter movement, the business case for diversity and inclusion is also now being understood.[15]

There is an imperative to recognise diverse identities, for example, across gender, LGBTQ+, race, generations, culture, sexuality, politics, religion, neurodiversity, physical ability and the many new ways in which people now identify themselves in the world of work. There are digital natives and non-natives, remote workers, transnational digital nomads, virtual assistants and contingent workers. To succeed, companies must recognise the enormous challenges ahead of them because they've not been faced with the need for a depth of diversity such as this, until now.

Neurodiversity: A Case Study of Missed Opportunity?

There are serious skill shortages in the rapidly expanding and strategically important sectors of data analytics and IT services implementation. Key to these sectors are tasks that are a good match with the abilities of some neurodiverse people. In the US, in 2017 only 37% of individuals with disabilities were in employment, compared to 79% for their non-disabled peers,[16] and neurodiverse talent forms a proportion of those left behind. One of the main reasons for this is that a standardised approach to recruitment – favouring qualities such as teamwork, communication, networking and the ability to conform to standardised practices and expectations – tends to systematically exclude those who are not neurotypical.

As a result, many companies are missing out on the benefits of recruiting neurodiverse talent: increased productivity, higher quality standards, greater innovation and overall improvements to employee engagement. Writing in 2017 for the *Harvard Business Review*, Robert D Austin and Gary P Pisano outlined how SAP, Hewlett Packard Enterprises (HPE), Microsoft, Willis Towers Watson, Ford and EY have been innovating with programmes that are inclusive of neurodiversity.[17] They list examples of the success of these approaches, such as how HPE's Australia-based neurodiverse testing team was shown to be 30% more productive than the others.

The article suggests steps that organisations can take to increase their neurodiverse intake. These include alternatives to interview-based assessment and training processes, support ecosystems once in the job and training for managers. The authors give this example of the culture and mindset shift required:

> SAP uses a metaphor to communicate this idea across the organization: People are like puzzle pieces, irregularly shaped. Historically, companies have asked employees to trim away their irregularities, because it's easier to fit people together if they are all perfect rectangles. But that requires employees to leave their differences at home – differences firms need in order to innovate.

The companies that are tailoring their approach to recruitment and management practices more effectively – in order to unleash the distinct capabilities of neurodiverse talent – are experiencing organisation-wide benefits. As Austin and Pisano point out, "The success of neurodiversity programs has prompted some companies to think about how ordinary HR processes may be excluding high-quality talent." In other words, companies where recruitment, cultural and management practices are following a standard template, without attempting to include wide-ranging forms of diversity, are missing out on the benefits.

Greater diversity of thinking will be needed in the 4.0 era, as well as a recognition of the importance of cultural fit. In the 20th century, we recruited to this model: a person's competence to do the job and ability to be up and running, contributing and performing as soon as possible. Companies such as Blonk, through its recruitment 'matching' app, and Your FLOCK, the culture improvement company, are taking a different approach. They are thinking more broadly and creatively around how best to get the right fit between candidate and company (be they permanent or contingent resource) and how to match an organisation's culture with people being recruited. This, in turn, is to ensure better alignment of the values and behaviours underpinning the company culture.

Blonk devised an app-based recruitment platform with a new matching algorithm inspired by Tinder! It reasoned that in a similar way to love matching, recruitment is about a more profound connection – beyond capabilities and into fit, culture and values alignment.[18]

Your FLOCK – a startup in Manchester, UK – is anchoring recruitment and retention strategy squarely with organisation culture and fit. It firmly believes that getting the right hire can provide stability, performance and longevity for all parties, avoiding a potential culture clash not evident in the job profiling and organisational 'promise' upfront.[19] It has since extended its app-based solution to define, check and enhance team cultures as a key component of organisational success and people engagement.[20]

For the first time in history, we'll have up to five generations working together. There will be challenges at each end of the spectrum. How do we engage and utilise baby boomers and generation X as they extend their retirement horizon and can contribute to the workplace for longer? How do we prepare our workplaces and existing workforce for the influx of generation Z; and how do we support generation Y – millennials – as they continue to climb the ranks and take on more senior management and leadership roles?

In addition to this already complicated situation, we must also consider what I call 'warm versus cold', which is the human worker versus the artificial or robot worker. This will become a real issue for many by 2030, as increasingly smart technologies and intelligences integrate as part of the workforce, not just the workplace.

Over the next 10 years, the global workforce will see significant growth in jobs in the tech and healthcare sectors (roles in construction, law and accountancy are also set to grow).[21] It is widely recognised now that innovation and creativity will form a major part of the 21st century human skill set.

The new era demands we encourage different thinking. Only then can we truly innovate, transform and become more flexible and agile. The more we can promote this freedom of thought, the more organisations who are struggling to transform from the traditional mould can emerge as bold, new 21st century businesses.

Companies That Are Getting It Right

In the digital era, speed is more important than size. There is no longer such a thing as 'too big to fail'. It's more likely that you'll be too slow to succeed.

"I worry about not being fast enough... There are just so many things to do, and speed is of the essence. And what's especially exciting about China is that you may be the best now, but if you're not fast enough, a 70% solution can beat you."

Jessica Tan, co-CEO, Ping An Insurance

The Chinese banking and insurance company Ping An is a great example of an organisation that is transforming from a traditional banking and insurance company to being a leader in insurtech and fintech. This embracing of the possibilities provided by digital adoption is enabling internal and external services, solutions, collaborations and partnerships that are driving unbeatable customer experiences, time and time again; ahead of any of their competition. Ping An has the mentality that a 70% solution can beat you, so speed is of the essence. The need for speed means that in the digital world we are becoming more accepting of failure, and understand that subsequent technical updates or versioning will improve an app or other online solution.

Notably, companies that were just starting or that didn't even exist in the 20th century are defining the landscape of the very early 21st – not only from the traditional west but from the east.

To illustrate the point, nine big-hitting companies are succeeding in the digital era. These could be called the trillion-dollar club, collectively ranking as one of the top 20 economies in the world today. This club is made up of Google, Amazon, Facebook, Apple, Microsoft, Xiaomi, Baidu, Tencent and Alibaba. They have changed the face of business and of life.

What is clear is that while the west has traditionally been dominant, we have now entered the Asian century, a term coined by the *Financial Times*.[22]

Asia is indeed rising, and Industry 4.0 is the catalyst that will change the landscape of business for the foreseeable future. The power base is shifting.

With this kind of firepower, organisations everywhere can find a new way to structure themselves, operate and transform for the current era. A big part of this will be to unleash the talent within businesses. Leaders at all levels can go beyond their job role and start to contribute strategically as much as operationally. Their time is now, and time for those who won't change is running out.

Beat the Ticking Clock

It used to take decades for a big company to fail, but at the current speed of business, it's now down to 18 months or less. This is why the five forces must be understood and tackled, quickly, by any company who still wants to be in business through the 2020s and beyond.

Without this understanding, we cannot truly engage and unleash the potential within our people. We cannot think about new, flatter structures for our organisations that would make leadership a more collective, measurable activity for everyone, not just the few. This is the age of empowerment and the organisations transforming and succeeding are those that combine the digital evolution of their businesses with a strongly empowered and trusted workforce of people encouraged to unleash their inner CEO, regardless of role or level, and contribute more strategically to the business, as much as across the day to day.

What Next?

So where to start? It feels like a huge task. We are trying to transform our organisations, embrace the digital revolution and unleash the power of our people, all at the same time. Here is the first of six interviews that accompany this book. These interviews bring in external thought leadership, existing best practices and examples of organisations getting it right (and wrong).

Our first interviewee, Johanna Bolin Tingvall from Spotify, would argue that the threshold of the Fourth Industrial Revolution is precisely the place whence great things can happen, including unleashing the empowerment and support of in-role CEOs.

INTERVIEW WITH
JOHANNA BOLIN TINGVALL

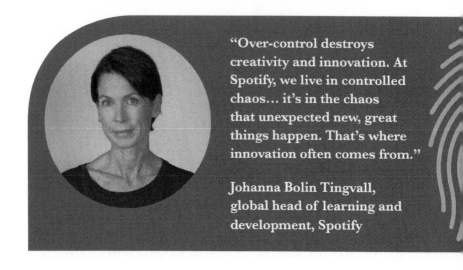

"Over-control destroys creativity and innovation. At Spotify, we live in controlled chaos... it's in the chaos that unexpected new, great things happen. That's where innovation often comes from."

Johanna Bolin Tingvall, global head of learning and development, Spotify

Johanna Bolin Tingvall is currently the global head of learning and development at Spotify, based in Stockholm, Sweden. Johanna has been at the forefront of HR and learning throughout her career and leads human capital development through GreenHouse, Spotify's internal learning and development function.

In this interview, Johanna explains how the development of built-in strategies for unleashing creativity and cross-business collaboration is enabling Spotify to innovate faster than its competitors. Spotify's flatter management culture plays a key role in empowering everyone in the organisation to contribute their ideas.

Jeremy

In the newer organisations, such as Spotify, as well as the transformed 20th century legacy businesses that are now evolving their business models, it is important to restructure, remove layers of hierarchy and empower people so leadership is unleashed throughout organisations. As we head into the 2020s and beyond, how important do you think it is to unleash leaders and leadership at all levels?

Johanna

With the ongoing development of technology, the world is moving much faster, and decisions are being taken at a speed never heard of before. Things change quickly, which means it is increasingly difficult to make decisions in the traditional bureaucratic way: with hierarchies and levels of management. It's just too slow.

So, the speed of change, speed of business, and the speed of evolving ways of working make it essential for all levels to be involved in decision-making. It's simply more efficient and productive – and more engaging.

Another consideration is innovation and how the pace of innovation is driven. You need to unleash the power of everyone's ability to come up with great ideas, much quicker and more efficiently than in the past. This way of working offers huge benefits because you get diverse ideas, which progress faster, as layers of red tape are removed.

I believe we need to empower everyone to take the lead and make informed decisions, supported by the business, to be able to keep ahead of the competition and constantly evolve.

Jeremy

If I can relate it to Spotify, a digital era business, how does this level of empowerment manifest itself to the benefit of the company and the individuals stepping up and taking ownership?

Johanna

With more autonomy to make decisions in any role, it moves us towards mutual goals and strongly engages employees as they own part of the journey. That has been an important way of operating at Spotify and we know that higher levels of engagement are directly correlated to productivity improvement.

Based on research, we know that autonomy – particularly having the ability to make our own decisions – is a strong motivator, and we see it every day. The added benefit is that people learn and grow faster the more autonomous they become, as the path will not be the same every time. Note that the autonomy does not mean 'you can do whatever you like all the time'; we do have goals to ensure that we are moving in the same direction. But we also have built-in ways of working for letting creativity loose.

For example, a few of our greatest ideas for new Spotify solutions, such as *Discover Weekly*, which is a weekly mixtape of recommended music tailored to each listener, have come out of this. *Discover Weekly* came from one of our hack weeks. It's a recurring time when we empower everyone to work together and focus on whatever they want. They can innovate anything. At the end of the week, a few of those things are taken forward and built into real solutions and services.

This creates a high level of engaged employees, and diverse creative solutions being created and implemented quickly. These are big benefits for any company getting it right.

Jeremy

How does this support career pathing if we use a traditional approach? Or does it drive something different?

Johanna

We don't have traditional career ladders because they don't work in Spotify's fast-changing environment. Instead, we talk about growth.

Someone who starts working with us may not get a new title every six months or a promotion, but they will have the opportunity to learn and grow. Even if their title is the same for two years, the job will not stay the same because it will constantly shift, change and throw up new challenges and opportunities to handle. It's the very nature of our Spotify environment. We encourage our band members to be inventive and to try new things. You grow yourself, and in turn, help to grow the company. We strongly believe in a growth mindset.

Jeremy

So, this is essentially the DNA of the organisation. Therefore, if we consider legacy 20th century businesses, looking to transform, do you think the Spotify blueprint is appropriate?

Johanna

To start with, I have the utmost respect for companies that have been around for a long time, with the challenge to transform. I believe the main benefits of digital transformation revolve around unlocking creativity and innovation, and to do that you need to be adaptable and nimble.

In addition, transformation that unleashes inner CEOs – self-leaders – will help people feel they can own their development, while contributing proactively and strategically to the growth of the company. This, in turn, leads to more engaged people who want to stay and grow in a more rewarding and enriching environment. I believe this approach is necessary to survive in today's business climate, whether you are a 21st century company or a transforming 20th century organisation.

Jeremy

I'd like to understand the conditions in place at Spotify for how the company encourages, empowers and engages its employees to take ownership and contribute beyond their job role. How do you ensure this happens effectively for both the individual and Spotify?

Johanna

One good example at Spotify is something we call 'bets'. All the business units have their objectives for the year, and they are aligned with the company targets, but then we also have the bets, the bigger projects – where we 'make a bet' on something, an informed guess – that require cross-business unit collaboration. These rely on different functions and teams working together. We get people from different parts of the organisation to form a bets team. We need buy-in to these bets and resources from all the business units. This is a way to minimise silos and increase cross-function, cross-business unit collaboration, separately from normal day-to-day operations.

The bet is not guaranteed to succeed and relies on the ingenuity, collaboration and creativity of the people involved. It's truly empowering and engaging. It's a great way to remove yourself from the day-to-day role and become part of a different coalition. This helps to unleash your inner CEO and become an active innovator.

Jeremy

This leads beautifully into the next piece, and possibly the most important catalyst for success. Many organisations talk about leadership at all levels but don't quite get it right.

Often this is because they are not built in a way to support it, structurally. It's not in their DNA or in their current mindset. For this reason, unleashing leadership requires a huge shift in thinking.

From your experience, what conditions have to be in place at C-level – culturally, and structurally – to enable people to safely and successfully unleash their inner CEO?

Johanna

The conditions have to be driven from the top. Spotify is by culture a rather flat company, but still, we have our CEO, Daniel Ek, who has set the scene here. We're a purpose-led company. Every member of the team knows where we're going and why, and we have a strong set of values to guide the way.

The main reason is that our CEO and the rest of the executive leadership team at Spotify are committed to building the core company purpose, having strong supporting values in place and enabling a very transparent company climate that builds trust. For this reason, people dare to try new things. An environment of trust drives the transparency that makes it possible for people to know what they can do and how they can contribute and have the confidence to participate in discussions.

I think that having a foundation built on solid purpose and strong values informs the culture. In essence, the kind of company we are and want to be, now and in the future. Of course, the culture will evolve, with each new person who joins the company.

Jeremy

How does this manifest itself in terms of how it feels to work and be a contributor at all levels at Spotify?

Johanna

It clarifies direction for the company and how we can all contribute inside and outside our job roles. I also think the flat hierarchy we have at Spotify is important. Of course, we're a growing company so we're adding layers, but our culture remains flat and consistent. We don't have the typical bureaucracy where if you have an idea, you have to go to your manager, then it has to go to the next level of managers. With us, if you feel your idea is strong enough, you can go straight to Daniel. We have open and transparent communication within the company. We've also put processes in place to support and reinforce it, such as providing internal communication channels, which make it easier to get access and to express yourself to the senior leaders in the company.

Jeremy

I've recently done a piece of research which highlights a major trend that within the next five years 40% of any organisation's workforce is likely to be made up of independent workers and contractors. We are seeing the rise of the blended workforce. So, if we're creating an empowering culture built on the DNA you've described, which has until now mainly been for our permanent employees, is this the same for our independent workforce and how would that work?

Johanna

We discuss that a lot at Spotify. When it comes to the way you do your job or your level of autonomy, we don't make a distinction between our permanent and non-permanent resources. We engage our independent workers and contractors in everything we do at Spotify, very openly. But of course, we observe the given laws in different countries.

Even when it's team development or transparency of information about what we're doing as a business. If it helps them do their job and contribute to Spotify's progress and growth, then it works for everyone. We're a transparent company and anyone who comes in, whether a contractor or a permanent employee, has access to practically all information through our internal communication channels. I've never been in an organisation that is this transparent and also a public company. It's hugely empowering, engaging and motivating for our workforce, whether they are permanent or independent workers.

Jeremy

When we look at the hard facts, does this drive as much mutual value between Spotify and its independent contractors, as it does with permanent employees?

Johanna

Yes, I see it work every day, but there are some differences. We may have a contractor filling an interim role for one year or someone coming in to deliver just one training session. So, of course, it differs. Overall, value is most effectively derived from our permanent resource, but there is strong value in the independent resources we use, and they are treated with respect and openness.

Jeremy

We have discussed the importance of unleashing inner CEOs, and the organisational culture and corporate leadership mentality that makes it happen, including how it impacts permanent and independent workers alike. As we empower people throughout the levels in our organisations, we can remove management layers and repurpose line managers to enable and support our unleashed inner CEOs. How should we repurpose the role of the line manager to empower people to do and be more?

Johanna

I think the line manager's role is still to do those things that glue the strategic direction of the business to the operational execution of the plan. It's also about reinforcing where we're going through our core purpose and goals. They can be close to the team and take part in the execution. They can also guide and manage the tasks and the people, so the individuals within the team produce what they need in the best way. So, it's being more of a coach like in sports, rather than the manager who tells people what to do and what needs to be achieved. A coaching mindset unlocks the power of line management and brings out the power of unleashed inner CEOs. This flourishes when managers don't micromanage and this, in turn, creates engaged managers.

Jeremy

It's been fascinating talking with you, Johanna, and I have just one more question. What is the cost for those companies that resist transforming into a modern, flatter organisation that truly empowers people?

Johanna

I believe the cost will be high if they can't find new ways of increasing innovation, engagement and speed within their companies. They will have a hard time attracting the talent they need, and they will most likely be left behind when it comes to innovation – meaning they will have a hard time keeping up with the competition.

It's about giving autonomy but also being clear about where we are heading. It's about giving people the right tools and skills so they can step up while being supported by line managers who have the time to guide and coach them.

We need some structure and a support network, but not too much. Overcontrol destroys creativity and innovation. At Spotify, we live in controlled chaos. We have the structure in place to avoid total chaos, but it's in the chaos that unexpected new, great things happen. That's where innovation often comes from.

Jeremy

What a wonderful way to conclude our discussion. I now have a new mantra in my head, "It's in the unexpected chaos that great things happen." I know some would find that shocking, when they reflect on their organisations, but being able to let go and unleash the power of inner CEOs to enable this magic is what this book is all about.

"This means we have more engaged people who want to stay and grow in a more rewarding and enriching environment... People feel they can own their development while contributing proactively and strategically to the growth of the company."

Johanna Bolin Tingvall

CHAPTER 2:

A New Approach for Changing Times

Introduction

It is a commonly held belief that in a world which focuses on increased cyber automation, there'll be fewer jobs and with that, higher unemployment. We witnessed the motor industry becoming fully robotic, and today we stand poised at the starting line of the motor industry's biggest revolution: the electric and autonomous vehicle age.

Long before the dawn of the first Industrial Revolution, Queen Elizabeth 1 publicly announced, "I have too much regard for the poor women and unprotected young maidens who obtain their daily bread by knitting, to approve an invention which, by depriving them of employment, would reduce them to starvation."[23] The queen was referring to a piece of technology which would make weaving more efficient and could do the job of three women. The fear factor was just the same as today.

New technology, innovation and thinking predictably trigger a fear of the change to come. Some people embrace and rapidly drive it, while others spiral into panic and respond as though it were a threat rather than an opportunity. We have been here before, and while change is more rapid in the Industry 4.0 era, the past can inform the future.

Fast-forward 300 years from Queen Elizabeth's statement, and it is apparent that automation was the absolute key to the growth and survival of the weaving industry. By the end of the 19th century, the cotton and weaving industries of Great Britain were increasingly automated and, notwithstanding the harsh conditions which improved only slowly, there were four times as many factory weavers as there had been in 1830.

Today, Jeff Bezos of Amazon understands how automation promotes the growth of employment. Amazon has increased the number of robots working in its warehouse facilities over the past three years from 1400 to 45,000. In its first three-year robotic era of growth, up to 2016, employment rose from 120,000 to 350,000 (excluding non-permanent workforce).[24]

As well as creating jobs, the digital era is fuelling an acceleration in creating customers. For example, it took the airline industry 68 years to attract 50 million users, electricity 46 years, television 22 years, cell phones 12 years, the internet seven years, Facebook three years, and Pokémon Go a staggering 19 days (yes, days). We can look at this in two ways: it's 19 days to competitive advantage or 19 days to failure. There is a fine line between success and failure in the 4.0 era, and it is speed that is the defining factor, not the size of a company as in the past. Speed to change, speed to action and speed to impact growth is the difference between winning and losing.

In the increasingly technologically enabled workplace, everyone needs to be able to adapt and integrate the digital with the human touch. There is an increased need to be tough on the relevant issues, rather than on individual personalities. Change is a constant, so displaying the ability to reinvent, change the game and change direction is needed all the more in this new era. It's essential to seek coaching and to coach others when they are struggling, as well as supporting those who are flourishing. A more collaborative and collective effort is required.

Unleashing the inner CEO within our organisations can create the advantage that is now essential in our changing times. In this chapter, the concept of the inner CEO and the key points involved in its unleashing are set out. It is relevant therefore for all audiences: executive leaders seeking to understand the strategic possibilities offered by unleashing CEOs; HR, organisational design and individual contributors. What follows is the broad scope of the inner CEO journey, and its implications at an organisational and a personal level.

More details on these different dimensions are provided in Chapter 3 (which focuses on leadership and culture shift), Chapter 4 (the organisational perspective) and Chapter 5 (the operational and personal level).

Within all this, we must acknowledge that change can bring fear, and fear can paralyse corporations into a self-destructive state of failure as much as being the catalyst for success. Winston Churchill is famous for saying, "Fear is the reaction, courage is a decision."[25]

With courage comes new opportunity, possibility and advantage, for those willing to learn how to think differently.

So, Some Definitions: Who or What Is the Inner CEO?

The inner CEO is that potential – within individual contributors at any level – to innovate, generate ideas and lead the plan into action, going beyond the boundaries of their day job, without having to stop and ask for permission.

The ability to collaborate with all levels as well as peer groups results in an increased degree of effectiveness and productivity. In this new era, people must not only be excellent at their individual job roles but must also make a strategic contribution to the business.

Who are In-Role CEOs?

In-role CEOs are those who have realised this potential, having unleashed their inner CEO. They are empowered to lead operationally and strategically, beyond their core role.

Unleashing inner CEOs, whatever their level, to become in-role CEOs, will herald a truly empowered workforce, backed by repurposed, supportive management lines and a leadership team that moves away from a reliance on 'command and control' and into a state of enablement.

Who is Responsible for Unleashing the Inner CEO?

Executive leaders, HR professionals and managers, as well as individual contributors all have a role to play in realising this potential. Executive leaders do so by creating a culture of empowerment and trust so that this potential is realised. HR professionals and managers can implement this culture and facilitate the development of individuals seeking to unleash their inner CEOs.

And of course, individual contributors play their part by stepping up, taking responsibility and being accountable for successful implementation while being supported by management as needed.

This vision is no longer the preoccupation of the executive leadership teams, boards or HR professionals; it can be owned by and become the responsibility of everyone. To fast-track action for everyone, I have developed a road map for success to unleash the inner CEO within our people and create engaged, empowered and performing in-role CEOs.

This has to start with a framework to articulate and assess the capability of those on the journey.

The 4Es Empowered Leadership Model for Unleashing In-Role CEOs: Envision, Engage, Execute and Excel

Each of the '4Es' is a critical step in assessing, developing and building the skill sets and traits required to excel as an in-role CEO. Developing in-role CEOs within the workforce will encourage executive leaders and managers to embed the right culture, and the innovative structures to sustain it. This will be key to driving a fast start, not a false start.

Figure 2: The 4Es Empowered Leadership Model

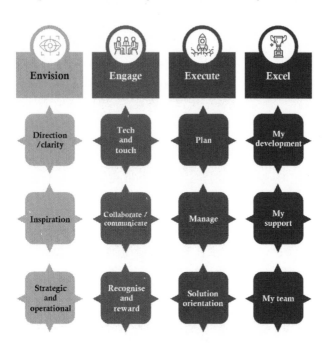

1. ENVISION

Those ready to unleash their inner CEO need to 'envision'. This comprises three key areas.

Direction and Clarity

Direction means to be able to clearly articulate the direction they aim to move in, whoever they are talking to, whether up the line, down the line or across lines. Questions to consider are:

- What is the goal?
- What does success look like?
- Is everyone clear what needs to be done?

Inspiration

The second is being inspirational. Individuals may have or think they have a brilliant idea, but if the ability to bring along others from up the line is missing, in terms of providing support for an idea, as well as a collaborative group to help in the execution of it, then the unleashed CEOs' projects may fail before they've begun.

Potential in-role CEOs need to act like leaders and be able to inspire others in their own distinctive way. Others in the company must also get behind the ideas generated and come along for the ride. This requires an ability to motivate and display a good balance of emotional intelligence (EQ) as well as the more traditional IQ.

I've found that what truly makes great (versus average) leaders is the emotional and personal side of the relationship. It's the ability to be more self-aware about how one is behaving, acting and impacting others in the organisation. Good questions for prospective in-role CEOs to ask themselves are:

- How do you manage yourself?

- How do you empathise with and motivate others, and how do you bring everybody together?

This is the type of leadership that makes a real difference. If you think of the best leaders you have worked with in your career, think about the traits that make them a great leader. It's not only that they hit their targets; it's typically more about the emotions you feel in your interaction with them. It's great to work with these leaders. There's a feel-good factor: a feeling that they get *you* and have got *your* back.

Strategic and Operational Outlook

And the third is the importance of having an eye to the sky and feet on the ground, which is a combination of the strategic and operational understanding.

The strategic component is a new idea or project that aligns to the direction of the overall business, contributing beyond job role, team and even function. It means considering how a new idea will impact the business. The operational component follows and focuses on what execution by in-role CEOs will look like, including the mobilisation of appropriate resources and support needed to implement the idea or project successfully.

I repeat: in-role CEOs have got to have both, not just the one. They have to think differently when considering the strategic and operational sides. It's a combination. An in-role CEO simply can't have one without the other. This is strategic, critical and creative thinking all rolled into one. There's a need to review progress, navigate the route, problem-solve and be flexible and adaptable as development progresses.

2. ENGAGE

The second component is the ability to 'engage' others, which is also made up of three key components.

Tech and Touch

The first part of engaging others on this journey of unleashing the inner CEO is knowing how to bring people along with you. This requires a strong personal touch, supported by enabling technologies to enhance communication, clarity and sharing. In-role CEOs must recognise that we are in the digital and dispersed age, an era where we have technologies at our fingertips which can enable success and increase efficiency and effectiveness. In-role CEOs have got to know which tools are appropriate and available, as well as being confident in using them. They have to be expert in the technology and tools they adopt, using them to enhance the human touch, helping to connect people in new ways, for closer co-working. This, of course, will undoubtedly require supportive training, coaching and skill development.

Collaborate and Communicate

We are entering an era of more collective leadership and this is enabling greater levels of collaboration and more open communication. Many individual contributors are already being asked to be part of cross-functional projects, as well as being encouraged, within their teams, to own tasks, objectives and goals together. More collaboratively and in a more coordinated way. The rise of self-driven or self-owned teams has been the mainstay in the technology sector for many years, leading to more agile methods of work: scrums, sprints and more. It's been more recently that other industries, teams, co-workers and so on have woken up to the power of collaboration.

Simply put, according to Jostle, the people connection company, "Collaboration in the workplace is what makes teamwork successful."[26] Winning and inclusive collaboration in the current era relies on two distinct factors:

- First, the digital technologies in place to enable it, driving more efficient communication, timely task management and improvement in overall productivity.

- Second, the all-important human touch, which is the glue that makes winning collaboration tick and stick.

Therefore, the digital and human combination elevates collaboration and communication to a higher level, which means that the execution of an idea can happen much faster. The in-role CEO needs to know how to communicate effectively and create strong, collaborative teams.

Recognise and Reward

The role of recognition and reward features just as heavily as it always has in leadership. People are more engaged when they are recognised for their efforts. This is an aspect of human touch that hasn't changed. Overall, a lot will be expected of newly empowered individuals in the future workforce, so how will the company reward this effort and contribution? What does it mean, and how will managers and leaders make sure it happens? How are in-role CEOs going to be rewarded for unleashing their inner CEO and embracing this new in-role leadership challenge?

This is an important conversation for every corporate leader, HR professional, line manager and individual contributor to be clear on. (See Chapter 4 for ideas about how organisations can recognise and reward in-role CEOs.)

In-role CEOs also have a responsibility when the people collaborating with them are doing an amazing job. So, it is important to consider their role in recognising the increased contribution from the wider workforce.

3.   EXECUTE

The third element requires an in-role CEO to be implementation-minded. There are three components central to success.

Plan

Successful execution requires planning. It's about having a good project management mindset and tools, as well as a good business planning foundation upon which to operate. Stakeholders must be engaged in a vision so that they can support the plan and sign it off.

Manage

Being able to manage the tasks and the key people in the team is central to steering the success of the project. Regular reviews and one-to-one sessions with the people involved will be required.

In-role CEOs must also be technically competent to manage a project timeline and use the appropriate technology and tools, which are constantly evolving.

Solution Mindset

It's essential to have what I call a 'solution mindset': knowing and accepting that there will be bumps and diversions along the way, while remaining focused on what is possible, rather than what can't be done. For in-role CEOs, this means thinking about how you can overcome problems quickly, escalating the problem when needed. It's about the ability to solve issues, mobilise the team to take rapid action and find a way forward to implement the plan and be successful.

4. EXCEL

The final component is 'excel', which is about the development of those individuals on this journey, as they unleash their inner CEO and demonstrate leadership. This consists of two essential parts: the personal development of in-role CEOs ('Me'); and their development as a collaborator and leader within the group ('We').

Me

The emotional intelligence we talked about comes into play here. It's about in-role CEOs asking themselves questions such as:

- Am I being the best I can be?

- Am I open, trusted and supportive of others?

- Am I aware of how I am operating and coming across to others?

- Am I going to do what I say, to execute and give it my all to be successful?

- What do I need to do, and to model, to excel in this brave new world?

This expansive, self-aware mindset is essential for in-role CEOs to excel while being part of the new, empowered organisation of the future.

This is explored further in Chapter 6, Measuring Employee Empowerment, through my new model, The Six Centres of Me. This is made up of six topics on which to reflect, so that we can measure the success of the personal side of unleashing our inner CEOs.

We

'We' means building a climate whereby in-role CEOs can work effectively with others, engaging them in the journey and motivating them to perform, as they contribute to the ultimate success of the project or task at hand.

To support this, in-role CEOs need to develop a coaching mindset to support individuals as they focus on getting the job done.

How do *we* work together as a high performing team? How do *we* focus on our goal to successfully implement the plan? It's about everyone in the team giving and asking for help where appropriate. In-role CEOs must model the desired behaviours and skills required and be prepared to support those who are on the journey with them.

How to Make It Happen

What needs to be in place to enable and empower individual contributors to unleash their inner CEOs, and realise their potential as in-role CEOs? There are four key areas in the process for robust identification and support of candidates who are ready to embrace the opportunity to become an in-role CEO:

- An empowering, supportive organisational and management structure (see Chapter 4)

- A way to recognise and reward performance for those unleashing their inner CEO and making progress (see Chapter 4)

- Assessment of potential candidates (see Chapter 5)

- A 90-day fast-start, measurable road map and development planner (see Chapter 5).

These four areas of my Empowered Leadership Model form a framework that involves many different stakeholders in the organisation. Executive leaders are positioned to set the framework and mindset of the organisation so that they are adopted wholeheartedly.

Bringing It All Together

The current era is bringing together the digital with the human touch. Some call it the phygital age.[27] An in-role CEO must have the ability to select and apply the appropriate technology to fit the purpose and use it to enable a high-touch way forward, enabling those accompanying them on the journey to collaborate, share and communicate effectively and efficiently.

How we operate in the digital era is critical. The technology and the human touch are inseparable, and one won't work without the other. Being cooperative and communication-minded is required to launch small, empowered, self-owned teams who manage themselves – supported by appropriate technology, not overwhelmed by it.

It's vital to encourage involvement, to review and communicate, and then talk some more. Team collaboration and communication are central to an in-role CEO's success.

The 4Es Empowered Leadership Model provides a framework for unleashed CEOs at all levels to develop the necessary knowledge, skills and behaviours that will define success and growth, individually and for the company. In Chapter 5, you will find a 90-Day Road Map that details this developmental journey.

With the 4Es model, the 90-Day Road Map provides an important structure for organisations to better manage, coach and measure the progress of the individuals who are stepping up and leading at all levels.

What Next?

In the next chapter, I will set out guidance for creating the right kind of culture that needs to be in place in order to realise this vision. Before that, in the second interview, Natasha Prasad talks about creating the right and safe environments for unleashed CEOs to thrive and how the potential in-role CEOs should be developed and nurtured by the organisation.

INTERVIEW WITH
NATASHA PRASAD

"Everyone has the potential to lead."

Natasha Prasad,
head of capability and
customer experience
Mambu

Natasha Prasad is currently head of capability and customer experience at fintech company Mambu, which operates a cloud platform for banking and lending businesses. Throughout her career in sales, service, human capital management and capability roles, Natasha has been passionate about empowering others, and providing them with a platform to perform and contribute beyond their core role. Natasha is driven by helping people to discover the best version of themselves, which is the theme at the heart of this book.

Jeremy

Why is driving leadership through the organisation – unleashing the inner CEO – important for today's businesses?

Natasha

These days, employees are looking to be empowered and recognised for their ability to achieve more, by accessing their broader knowledge, passions and skills to contribute above and beyond their job role. Organisations need to encourage a mindset of curiosity so that unleashed leaders can fail fast, learn, succeed and grow. A 'growth mindset' is about everyone having the potential to step up, and the impact on business growth is huge.

To have a vibrant workforce, organisations must attract and keep the right talent, as well as allowing people to take on leadership activities, whether self-based, team-based or task-based leadership. I believe everyone has the potential to lead even as an individual contributor. We just have to allow them to step up and shine. A simple example would be a high-performing team and how they rotate individual contributors to chair and lead meetings. Everyone gets a chance to step up, curate the agenda and reach out to people before the meeting to ask what the top challenges are that they wish to solve in the team meeting. It's a way to encourage people to step up as leaders and for them to test how it works in a safe environment.

Jeremy

In terms of actually making it happen, what does the leadership and management mindset need to be, to drive actions to unleash and support inner CEOs?

Natasha

From a leadership perspective, I mentioned growth mindset, which I believe is critical. This consists of having leaders who make it OK for you to test, learn, grow, develop and contribute in bigger, bolder ways. The leaders need to create the conditions for unleashed inner CEOs to learn from their challenges and take another shot, and this must be backed up by the right climate in the business, so they feel safe to push boundaries. I've found that the practice of psychological safety provides the ideal framework to unleash inner CEOs and embrace leadership at all levels. When people feel safe, and when the leaders trust their people, this nurtures a healthy exchange of ideas and collaboration. It's about knowing you won't be punished for having a go, but will be supported and able to learn from your experiences.

When this starts at the top with the leaders embodying this spirit, it speeds up the process and enables others to do the same and to be supported. Everybody contributes, and everyone grows.

Jeremy

What happens when this doesn't work; when there isn't a safe environment to own leadership at all levels?

Natasha

A good example of this is what happened with a high-performing colleague in an organisation where I worked. She was incredibly smart and such a good operator, but she was surrounded by a couple of alpha males who had been excellent salespeople and then promoted into sales leadership roles. They had not been given formal training around leadership styles and management practices, how to flex their styles to different situations, when to be directive and when to be consultative. They were out for the glory, and it was their team who would help them realise their dreams and bonuses, rather than the other way around.

It became command and control, and I witnessed it playing out around me. My colleague felt bullied and there were no psychological safety protocols to allow her to share her ideas, volunteer to lead tasks or contribute beyond her job role.

Any attempt to do so was seen as a threat by her bosses, rather than an opportunity to unleash her inner CEO.

It's such a shame because I have seen this happen so many times, across many different businesses with leaders who think it's a sign of weakness not to be at the front. They are blinkered, so they miss the people in their team with the potential to be and do more. The net impact is that these people will typically look for other roles because they think that if they're not appreciated, and it isn't a safe environment for them to spread their wings, then there's no point in them staying. It's such a waste at a time when talent is gold and the need for everyone in the business to step up is at its highest. I'd like to say these attitudes I've experienced are old-fashioned and rare, but sadly they are all too familiar. They are dangerous for the future health and growth of our businesses and people.

Jeremy

It's harder to convince many 'traditional' business leaders of the need for a flatter structure, empowered people and a new approach to how we manage. What do we need to do to support their journey, creating a safe climate to truly unleash the inner CEOs in organisations?

Natasha

I'm trying to solve this problem for myself because it is the challenge that human capital professionals encounter. They need to provide these leaders with support on the 'what': what leadership at all levels looks like, what a supporting executive body and line management need to do to reinforce and embody it, and what needs to happen to create an evidenced, safe environment for people to embrace the concept and to step up. We have to be consistent as a global company, and that is down to the leadership of the overall business. Leaders can make small changes that create a significant positive impact, for example, by aligning the language they use as well as the role they play to support unleashed inner CEOs.

I want to create a leadership level peer network so that as we evolve as an organisation, it's safe for our executive leaders and managers to step out of their comfort zone and drive the same spirit through the rest of the company. I know I need to help take the more traditional-thinking leaders in our company on a journey to what great leadership looks like in an age of transformation, with the recent pandemic and the way in which our workforce is evolving. We must get it right at executive leader level first for it to work across the rest of the organisation, because otherwise it will fail.

Jeremy

The obvious follow-up question for me is: what is it like in the companies that do get it right?

Natasha

In those companies that get it right, you see and hear people articulating how much they love working for their organisation because they genuinely feel valued and can make a difference. They say that there are plenty of opportunities, and they are recognised and rewarded appropriately for their contribution. They become brand ambassadors for life, even if they leave. When companies achieve this, having employees and ex-employees advocating for them, it speaks volumes for the brand in the marketplace. It attracts talent to come and work for the company, and they have a better chance of keeping them after their first motivated and energised 90 days, which is traditionally when commitment drops off. Having a great employee experience is central to employee engagement, commitment and retention of talent; it creates competitive advantage in human capital terms.

Jeremy

If we consider these types of companies you describe – empowering, engaging and productive, with everyone contributing – what are the benefits for the senior managers of those businesses?

Natasha

Senior managers are freed up to do what they were hired to do: to focus on the strategic direction of the business, anticipate market shift, clear roadblocks, build networks and connections, and ensure that the foundations are in place for consistent levels of winning strategy execution.

So many companies don't get it right: they talk the talk but don't walk the walk. I see a lot of leaders being too operational, which is driven by a lack of trust in their teams. They sit there giving orders, and then as soon as their people start to have a go, they criticise and control them.

Senior leaders who are more courageous, who acknowledge and recognise that there are plenty of people with the right attitude and skills to step up, and who can loosen the reins, empower others and accept there will be some experimentation, will realise the benefits almost immediately. For this to happen, the organisation needs to support its managers to become better coaches who protect and reinforce the strategic messaging, while delivering results through their newly empowered, stronger teams.

Jeremy

Can you give me an example of this going wrong in businesses?

Natasha

In one of the companies I worked for, my line manager had been with us for only five months. The company was relatively young, an ex-startup in its second phase of growth, which posed challenges. My line manager, [who was also] the head of sales and a senior leader, had a list of 60 projects on the go, as well as his management role. It was very operational, and his time was not being invested in strategy. I tried to reverse mentor him about simple things such as prioritising, focusing and delegating to help him take a step back to see the mostly unsurmountable tasks he had on his plate.

As one of his lieutenants, I tried to free him up so he could focus on the strategic direction in his function, which was sales. When the strategy in sales is not driven, it becomes tactical and short term; we needed to patch the holes that the fuzzy strategy and piecemeal execution had created, which was not sustainable. There was a ripple effect, with many leaders running around being tactical because the structures were not in place for the phase of growth. It looked positive, and no one was shaking the tree to warn of the issues ahead.

When I came in, one of the things we had to tackle was the need for internal decision-making around policies and procedures, and from a sales function perspective within our expanding customer base. For example, a simple question that remained unanswered for months, was, "Should we have a key account management function?" Why would talent come and why would talent stay with directionless leadership, which didn't create an empowering or enriching environment? The rest of us became immobilised and increasingly frustrated, and that's not a great place to be, especially not in a growth phase. It was no wonder my boss had so many projects on the go; he was patching the leaks and treating symptoms, not root causes. Leaders were focused only on short-term successes and hitting the numbers, which was frustrating. And for me, the obvious question unsurprisingly became, "Why should I stay here?"

Jeremy

What is your experience of an organisation that does encourage leadership at all levels for people to unleash their inner CEOs?

Natasha

In one company, I organised a workshop specifically for people we had identified to step up and contribute more to the business, beyond their job role. The intention was to get them to articulate what their future world could look like if they were more empowered and supported to be and do more. They created their future role, defined what success looked like and captured it all in a vision for their future selves. From the vision, I encouraged them to design their objectives and measurables by creating dashboards that would clearly record progress and highlight possible next steps and actions. After this, they all presented their ideas and structured thinking to the executive leadership team. This was a crucial step in their empowerment to step up and unleash their inner CEOs and embrace their roles and the possibility to achieve more.

The best participants were then sponsored to execute their plans immediately, and their line managers and I supported them.

What followed engaged everyone in the organisation. People said, "We can do this, and they will support us." It started with mental acceptance, driven by leadership behaviour, which leads to action. People flourishing depends on whether behaviour is supportive or creates barriers.

Jeremy

Let's say we've got the right conditions and are unleashing our inner CEOs. How do we catch people doing it right, driving the proper recognition and reward, on top of what they're getting paid for in their role?

Natasha

That's a great question and one that is not at the forefront of all leaders' minds when they are empowering others. When I've had outstanding leaders in the past, they've been brilliant at positive public recognition and constructive private recognition. They would catch people doing it right in front of others, and also help them with private coaching when they needed assistance or developmental feedback.

When we catch our unleashed in-role CEOs doing it right, there are so many things we can do to keep them energised, motivated and recognised. It's a combination of the line manager and senior sponsors, and the culture of the organisation and 'how they do things'. Pay increases and bonuses, team recognition, development opportunities, secondments, a 'well done' in front of the CEO, peer recognition and team outings can be put in place. This is where HR needs to own the execution by supporting unleashed inner CEOs to succeed at every step. The less obvious thing is curating interesting experiences for them, whether it's a mental challenge, project task or team challenge that is strongly aligned to their target or is focused on a skill set they're trying to develop. The positioning is one of recognition of what we believe they can achieve and how they will be rewarded for their contribution.

"From a leadership perspective, it's a growth mindset which I believe is critical, as this consists of having leaders who make it OK for you to test, learn, grow, develop, and contribute in bigger, bolder ways."

Natasha Prasad

CHAPTER 3:

Creating the Right Conditions to Unleash Inner CEOs

Introduction

It is imperative we adapt and reinvent ourselves to stay alive and thrive because success in business yesterday is not a guarantee of success in business tomorrow. Company failure during an industrial revolution is to be expected; however, Industry 4.0 in this new digital era has grown sharp, decisive teeth capable of despatching any business to close its doors in record time if it fails to adapt. David S Rose, entrepreneur and angel investor, said, "Any company designed for success in the 20th century is doomed to failure in the 21st."[28]

Conversely, companies that have already embraced transformation have created new roles in their organisations, such as chief digital officers (CDOs) and cyber risk managers, to consolidate and further build on change. These roles didn't exist 10 years ago. When designing the future workplace, there's a need to be optimistic rather than fearful. Change is a certainty, but it's also clear that more new roles will be created in companies that are not afraid to innovate.

This chapter is relevant to all but is essential reading for executive leaders looking to create a cultural and an organisational shift geared to empowering and unleashing inner CEOs.

Unleashing the Inner CEO: A Culture and Mindset Shift

Unleashing the inner CEO within identified members of the organisation is a huge shift. The change is about people moving from being almost entirely operational to becoming more strategic. Furthermore, it's about understanding the importance of their contribution to the company as a whole, as opposed to focusing on each person's role and day-to-day tasks.

Our organisations and workforce are changing fast. The most successful companies have already, or soon will, attempt to flatten their hierarchies and structures to empower people and give them greater autonomy. People throughout the organisation need management and leadership skills because the new way of working demands that these traits are demonstrated, no matter what their level may be.

Organisations are removing the old, restrictive hierarchies so that they can better unleash human potential in their companies. In practical terms, 'flattening structures' means removing lines of hierarchy. It entails stripping away the red tape and bureaucracy to enable people to innovate and make decisions whatever their current position, rather than continually deferring to layers of management above.

Leadership should no longer be the exclusive domain of those promoted into management roles. To unleash leadership potential, it's essential to embrace a sense of empowerment, and take ownership, whether a challenge is directly relevant to the role and whether it requires others to contribute. Our unleashed, in-role CEOs will be required to mobilise others, and themselves, to collaborate and communicate with greater degrees of clarity and direction, so that they can implement the actions necessary to accomplish the desired outcome.

When we unleash the inner CEO in key members of the workforce, we equip them to contribute to the ultimate performance of the company, in parallel with their job role must-do tasks. They take control not only of their tasks but of wider actions that will contribute to team and organisational performance, whether internally or externally focused. This contributes to the health of the whole business, from a company perspective and in the eyes of the customer.

The necessary action orientation is one of collaboration, to achieve the maximum possible with others, rather than operating with a tunnel-vision approach that adheres solely to an individual job description. Members of the evolving workforce can't allow themselves to be held back by fear of failure, or they will inevitably fail. To take ownership and achieve more, they must be supported and equipped to take calculated risks so they can contribute and grow.

Successful companies of the future must train their workforces to unleash their inner CEO, so that they are empowered and prepared to take ownership. Typically, they will need their people not only to upskill, but also to think differently. For most people, unleashing their inner CEO requires a dramatic shift in attitude from the traditional employee mindset. It's up to executive leaders to create the conditions of psychological safety, inclusion, trust and empowerment so that their people can embrace this mindset themselves and unleash their inner CEOs.

Enabling Leadership in the Digital Era

Let's look at the various components for considering what's required to lead from any level, in this new age. As we now know, digital transformation leads to whole-business transformation because to be fully digitally enabled we understand that the culture must also change. It's a state of mind. The right integration of technologies is needed, but at the same time, people must be mindful not to be blindsided by the digital. The challenge is how to unleash human potential when workers are more technology-enabled and increasingly based remotely, either as permanent employees or as independent workers. And the challenge for many in the digital era is not the technology itself, but the sheer pace of change.

With the introduction of smartphones in 2007, change accelerated at a speed not anticipated. This speed of change ushered in an age of disruption, in which established ways of doing things were challenged. New players in well-established industries suddenly were able to think differently and create something totally new, all enabled by the most appropriate technologies. Dynamic companies such as Amazon, Airbnb and Uber seemingly gained market leadership overnight, and there was no rule book for many of the more traditional companies caught in their wake to react fast enough. Since 2007 this has become a common feature of unprecedented disruption.

Let's say you're a traditional firm. How do you navigate the future? What are the things you need to do? How do you transform your organisation to compete in a new way that you didn't even know existed until now? There's the digital thread as well as the human thread to consider. Then there's the new blended workforce. You may have permanent employees, independent workers and so-called digital nomads, all contributing to your business.

What are the new rules of the road in terms of management and performance? You've also got a new generation joining the workplace as well as an ageing population at the other end. How do you get the best out of your human resources? One way is to encourage leadership at all levels in the organisation. A collective, committed approach to organisational health and success, at a time when change is a constant, and disruption is just around the corner. At times like this, you need everyone to step up and be part of the solution. A bigger risk is to revert to power being in the hands of a few executive leaders. In times of transformation and disruption this is an increasingly risky strategy, as perspectives may be narrow, and new thinking not a welcomed trait.

Companies such as Kodak, Toys R Us, Lehman Brothers and Blockbuster Video suffered. Organisations such as DBS Bank, Amazon, Citi, Alibaba and others have had more enlightened leaders, who have readily acknowledged that the power of the many trumps the power of the few, or the one. They embedded a more collective approach to how their companies needed to evolve, how decisions could be fast-tracked, with everyone involved; and they enabled the wider sharing of responsibility for success across functions, levels and borders. Leaders at all levels, everywhere, owning a part of the ultimate organisational success.

Everyone has the potential to unleash their inner CEO, but not everyone will, for whatever reason. With this in mind, future recruitment will need to be more focused on finding people who are ready and willing to take ownership, whether as permanent employees, freelancers or digital nomads. The new blended workforce will require people to demonstrate the traits of an independent worker, no matter where they are based or how they are contracted.

Empowering the whole workforce now ensures we have the distinctively human skills of innovation, strategy and leadership needed for the future, especially as many operational roles are likely to be automated[29] as we go further into the 2020s and beyond.

This need for self-leadership also impacts executive leaders, who must adapt their old leadership style to reflect the new workplace. This is not about 'losing' their power: this is about distributing ownership for strategic and operational success, so that they can focus on navigating the future direction of the company, supported and driven by a motivated, empowered and committed business.

The Inner CEO – a Strategic and Operational Balance

Traditionally we have looked at an individual's contribution as being mainly or purely operational, but now we're asking them to step up in this transformed, potentially flatter organisation and take greater ownership. Therefore, there is a need for an appreciation of the strategic side of things.

To realise their leadership potential, people need to understand the organisation's direction and have a route map to get to their goal. The operational side then entails being able to execute and to implement. It's steering towards success and bringing others along with them, and this requires a combination of the digital and the human resource. It's a collaboration of people and their unique skill sets. When people are digitally enabled with the right tools and know how to use them at a strategic level, it makes them far more productive at the operational level. Increased productive working allows a focus on both the strategic and operational, a central trait of our unleashed inner CEOs.

Our in-role CEOs must keep their eyes to the sky and their feet on the ground. At the strategic level, having their eyes to the sky means they need to be constantly tuned in to the course they are on and how their role contributes to the business direction as a whole. They must be alert to any changes that are liable to get in the way. They must possess, or develop, a keen appreciation of what makes the company tick internally, and an ability to mobilise resource and collaborate with stakeholders. At an operational level, they must have their feet on the ground because it's critical to know what's happening internally and externally as actions are implemented, business is driven and connections are made. In this respect, whether or not they have a customer-facing operational role is irrelevant. Ultimately, a company wins or loses by selling products and services, and by creating a positive experience for customers in the marketplace. The future workforce will be made up of those who are unleashed and empowered, rather than worker drones who are committed solely to ticking off their to-do list for their job.

People at every level will need coaching and training to understand and embrace this mammoth operational and mental shift. They will need new skills and behaviours to transform the organisation and themselves. They will need to be supported by a thoroughly committed executive leadership team, a flatter structure and line managers who embrace a growth mindset, as expressed in the interview with Natasha Prasad (see Chapter 2).

You may be thinking that the new era requires everyone to be a superhero. In some ways, this is true. The good news is that it's possible for everyone to be more engaged and empowered. It simply takes a willingness and desire to wake up, recognise and develop these core traits that we all possess and are built into the settings of our human potential. It starts with attitude; it becomes part of the organisational DNA and culture and enables those willing to step up to do so safely, with controlled risk and with support from an equally motivated and refocused management team.

The Traits of an In-Role CEO

There are certain traits an in-role CEO must display. I look for these traits when developing this new leadership at all levels in the organisations I work with, to guide them through this shift.

I see potential leaders everywhere and at every level. These people are already always looking ahead, as well as being in the now. It's a delicate balance between protecting the short term and what they need to achieve, while being future-minded about what they need to do next. It's like being a more operational chief executive officer.

Many organisations have got themselves into trouble in recent years because they have been too short-term in their vision, given the pressures of the market. As a result, they're now struggling with a lack of preparedness for the dynamic era we've entered.

An in-role CEO can liaise at all levels comfortably, internally and externally. This may take practice for many who have not been used to displaying or encouraged to show this kind of initiative.

The successful employee of the future must also take calculated risks, with the support of management, because this is going to be increasingly important. They must be able to communicate and sell their ideas in terms of developing the business case. To enable this, an important question for in-role CEOs to ask themselves is, "How do you engage others in the journey so you can execute successfully and be supported in striving for better solutions and innovation?"

It is vital that potential in-role CEOs are not set up for failure. They must be given the means to implement their ideas and to have a mobilised team around them. They need to be empowered, with a support infrastructure in place around them to accelerate success and growth. Executive leaders must set their in-role CEOs up for success and help them to create early wins. Superior leadership skills are still paramount, but the difference senior leaders can create lies in seeing everyone as having the potential to unleash their inner CEO, rather than confining individual contributors within their job description. And this includes not just the permanent workforce but the more blended workforce of the digital era. The blend is the mix of an empowered permanent and independent workforce, working together and taking ownership for the ultimate success of the company – as well as working within their job role.

That is why the evolving workplace offers a much more exciting opportunity for independent thinkers: those who remain within a corporate structure and those who choose to leave and be self-employed. In the new diverse workforce, these people will be able to enjoy more freedom in decision-making and creativity, be they permanent or independent workers. The time is ripe for recruiting and harnessing the abundant talent already available within and outside corporate confines. We no longer have to be constrained by a traditional permanent workforce and can explore more creative operating models and ways of working. The aim is to unleash in-role CEOs at all levels in our organisations, who contribute to strategic and operational growth. Independent workers not directly employed by your organisation have not traditionally been the beneficiaries of this kind of sponsorship. But this is not a time for a traditional approach. Wherever the talents of independent and flexible workers are helping drive your organisation forward, assisting them to unleash their inner CEO will nurture their loyalty and commitment.

There are a few considerations executive leaders should think through, in creating the conditions to successfully unleash the inner CEOs in their organisations. Here are the 12 decisive questions that I would urge boards, non-executive directors and executive leaders to work through.

The Decisive Dozen

1. Is the company, and am I as a senior leader, ready for this?

2. How do we ensure aligned attitudes and behaviours at executive leadership level, which will be needed to sponsor and support unleashing the inner CEOs in the organisation?

3. How do our current company values and behaviours need to evolve, to create the right culture for a new age of genuine empowerment in our organisation?

4. How high is the trust level in our organisation when considering the perception of our executive leadership team and management?

5. How will we create the conditions that will allow individual contributors to step out of their comfort zone and unleash their inner CEO?

6. What role will HR play in owning and supporting this process for our workforce (permanent and independent workers alike)?

7. How do we create a solid foundation of psychological safety to enable experimentation, openness, risk-taking and willing collaboration?

8. How do we as the executive leadership team 'catch people doing it right' and sponsor further those making rapid progress?

9. What new reward and recognition elements will have the biggest impact when our people unleash their inner CEO, make progress and succeed?

10. What are the new rules of the road, processes, learning paths and supporting infrastructure that we need to enable a truly empowered and often distributed workforce?

11. What are our measures for success and how will we know we are making progress?

12. How does this become the 'way we do things around here'?

Dr Amy Edmondson, the Harvard professor and scholar who coined the term 'psychological safety',[30] described this concept as, "a belief that one will not be punished or humiliated for speaking up with ideas, questions, concerns or mistakes". This belief is fundamental to the culture of experimentation, trust and boldness that leaders must establish. It must be in place in order to unleash in-role CEOs to thrive and inspire others, at both an operational and strategic level.

What Next?

In the next chapter, we'll explore what's needed to flatten the hierarchy to enable people to unleash their inner CEO and embrace in-role leadership.

Before that, our next interview features the point of view of Steen Puggaard, executive board member, equity investor and CEO.

INTERVIEW WITH
STEEN PUGGAARD

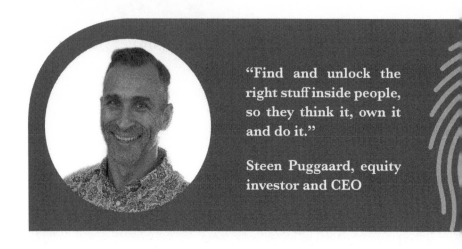

"Find and unlock the right stuff inside people, so they think it, own it and do it."

Steen Puggaard, equity investor and CEO

Steen Puggaard has supported and started many successful businesses, including the 4Fingers Crispy Chicken food chain. He was an early investor in and former CEO of the business, which he grew from one outlet in Singapore to several across the region, with a revenue of more than $40m annually, bucking the trend for how fast food could be provided and managed.

From the outset, Steen was committed to unleashing leadership at store levels and appointed, from day one, 'mini-CEOs' as he calls them. His executive leadership perspective on the importance of doing this, on empowering his people and protecting his own focus, provides great insights. This interview provides inspiration for leaders considering the questions concerning organisational culture and processes raised in the previous chapter.

Jeremy

Tell me about the qualities needed to be a successful entrepreneur and CEO, and how that relates to unleashing the inner CEO in the broader workforce?

Steen

My conclusion is that many people think that being an entrepreneur is a skill set you can learn, but I think it's more of a disposition or mindset.

In my experience, you need to have three fundamental qualities within you:

1. You need to be a little bit paranoid so that you're on your toes all the time, trying to anticipate what could happen next and who's coming at you from behind.

2. You need a thick skin. The reason I say that is because when you start a company, there will likely be a lot of rejection and failures along the way. If you're not able to find some sense of pleasure, enjoyment or motivation in the adversity, you will struggle to succeed.

3. You need to be obsessive. This allows you to be completely embedded and immersed in what you do so it becomes your mission and purpose in life rather than just an occupation.

These are the three qualities I applied when I took over and led the 4Fingers Crispy Chicken business, which at the time had great potential but was held back by shareholder disputes, poor management and lack of funding. You've got to figure out who you are first and what makes the business tick because if you do not start with establishing this first, you may work hard at your business, but not achieve success.

On the question of how it relates to unleashing the inner CEO in the broader workforce, I think it's necessary first to identify who has the right stuff to become a leader. That is a good basis for helping select those who can contribute to the business and team.

Jeremy

Let's take 4Fingers as an example. You clearly identified people who can unleash their inner CEOs and contribute to the broader business success, beyond their job role. How did you go about creating the environment for this mindset to flourish? .

Steen

The starting point was to instil in people the sense that we're all in charge of our own destiny. No one's going to do this for you. No one's going to make your bed. You are in charge of your own path. I gave people a very clear vision and a sense of where we were going, how we were planning to do it and what I expected from them, including how I'd ensure they were supported. This was a big motivating factor, and we reached a place where I could say to them, "Conquer that hill," and I knew I could rely on them to do it.

This is exactly what you need as a business leader: people at all levels who unleash their inner CEO, and back up their intent with successful action. I admire that. But it is a journey, and some people won't make it. That's why it is so much about the right stuff that is already within people, underpinned by upskilling and a willingness to grab opportunities, even when the going gets tough. The people knew what we were aiming for and what their contribution needed to be, so they could ask me and their managers for the resources to unleash their inner CEO and contribute beyond their role. At that point, the leadership team's job is to provide the environment and the tools they need so they can execute the vision.

In most cases, at 4Fingers, that worked well. I even used the term mini-CEO, rather than saying 'restaurant general manager'. It sowed different aspirations in people to think it, own it and do it.

I told my team, "I want you to aspire to have my job one day." I made sure that if people worked hard and contributed well, they could make it in the company. I really believed in bothering my mini-CEOs as little as possible, once they knew the direction and what was expected. That way, it was easy to spot who stepped up.

Some people didn't get it and saw a 'title', and with that they assumed entitlement. They didn't see the need for the mini-CEO state of mind, backed up by an evolving skill set and the need to deliver results above and beyond their job role.

Jeremy

What interests me is that you were able to unleash the inner CEOs at 4Fingers, even in the more constrained environment of fast-food service outlets. Outlets have to be consistent and repetitive in what they do and how they do things. You created a framework for this to happen within the scope of your business. It tells us that it's possible even in regulated, compliance-led, niche, cookie-cutter industries. What do you think?

Steen

I absolutely agree. Once you know what your business is about at its simplest level, you can build around it and create broader opportunities for people to contribute.

When I think back to 4Fingers, we built a business that went from zero to over $40m in just a few years. You do that by doing your core business well, consistently, and then building on it with uniqueness, great people and new ideas.

The core business was relatively simple, and I always said we needed to do two things excellently:

- Firstly, on a macro level, you figure out what it takes to run one store successfully. We asked questions such as, "How do we build it? How do we prepare? How do we staff it? What does the customer journey look like?" And then you document that really, really well. The rest is just scaling up as you add new outlets and concepts; you follow the cookie cutter.

- Secondly, you find out what it takes to serve one customer really well, and then you scale it up and strive to improve continually on that customer journey.

Going back to what we covered before: me, the CEO, saying to a store manager who was running one store, that they are a mini-CEO, is the assumption that they just had to figure out how to run one store well and how to serve one customer a day. I was at the top of all the stores, with each one of my mini-CEOs directly below. It removed the need for layers of management and empowered them to a much higher degree than was the case in the traditional businesses I've been part of.

What we did in 4Fingers may not be something you can replicate in all companies, but the philosophy is there as a guide. Empower others, put the required measures in place, and support them when they need it.

Jeremy

As a leader, what must be in place at the team leadership level to enable an environment where people embrace what you're saying and unleash their inner CEO?

Steen

First of all, the person in charge: the company's CEO needs to profoundly buy into the philosophy. Otherwise, it will never work. Back in the 80s, there was the fantastic turnaround story of Scandinavian Airlines. What happened is something I've applied many times. In fact, it still inspires the way I run businesses today. The company had been heading towards potential bankruptcy for a number of years: oil crises, cross-airline competition and so on. The board, in a last-ditch attempt at a turnaround, decided to bring in an outsider to the traditional airline industry for a different perspective. They approached Jan Carlzon, who ran a charter travel agency. He would charter planes and sell tickets to popular holiday destinations.

Scandinavian Airlines asked him if he would run the company. His immediate response was that he didn't know anything about airlines. They told him they wanted new ideas. He took the job and the first thing he did was to round up the head office staff in one of the aircraft hangars. He brought in a portable aircraft stepladder, climbed it and introduced himself as their new CEO. He confessed that he didn't know anything about running an airline, but he knew that they all did and that he was looking forward to receiving everyone's suggestion for how to improve the business!

My understanding is that the gist of what he said was that they were the ones facing the issues and therefore were the best people to find solutions. Importantly, he said that he was committed to empowering and supporting them. He gave an example of how he would push discretion out where it belonged. He said that if a passenger showed up late for check-in, rather than seeking permission from up the chain of command, they would instead have the authority to resolve the problem and to check the passenger in on the next flight at their discretion.

In essence, what he did was empower people at the pain points, at every level, where they faced the day-to-day challenges. I set out to do the same; I empowered my team but made it clear that I didn't want to be disappointed. I believe you have to add some pressure to truly empower people and appreciate how some of them grab hold of ownership. For me, as an empowering CEO, I prefer to give people trust so that they in turn have an opportunity to show me that they know how to handle it and deliver results. That's the way I do it. And when people live up to your trust, you should reward, recognise and empower them further.

Jeremy

It's empowering when the CEO models the right behaviour. You have leaders and managers in different functions, responsible for strategy execution. What needs to happen at line management level to commit to CEO role modelling, taking ownership and empowering others?

Steen

My ability to build any company depends on my ability to go out and attract the right people. I suppose I have the gift of the gab in terms of getting people excited. When you can engage people in the journey, excite and help motivate them, it's half the battle. To back that up, I walk the walk. I don't just talk the talk. It's genuine and evidenced every day as 'the way we do things around here'.

This is key because when you get your people to commit, they bring their intellect and their heart to the job. It's the winning combination where you can really see people operating on a clear personal mission in the organisation's direction.

My approach to recruiting leaders and managers is to spend time identifying and attracting those who I believe are giants for the company's situation, now, and who can steer success as it grows and grows in the future. The willingness to take ownership at any level inspires people to unleash their inner CEO and strive for brilliance. The business becomes a place where people show up because they want to and because they feel part of something larger than themselves.

Jeremy

That demonstrates the importance of having this very strong, open-minded leadership and empowering culture, doesn't it?

Steen

Someone once said that if you don't intentionally shape your company culture, culture will tend to shape itself. I adapted that mantra to suit my way of working. When I build a culture dedicated to excellence and to people working together, it runs itself. I don't need to watch things because I know that everyone is working towards the same goal and they're supporting each other.

When I launched Costa Coffee in Singapore, we were up against 120 Starbucks outlets and many other global, regional and local brands. I said, "The only way we can make this company take off is by a commitment to customer service and to product quality." This is not the stuff from manuals; it works because you believe in what you're doing. I looked into where the customer touch points were and realised it was the baristas who were the central pillars to winning over customers and ensuring long-term success. To me, they were not just people who operated coffee machines. They were heroes, creating experiences beyond a cup of coffee for our customers. We just had to unleash their inner CEOs.

I didn't know how to do it, but from a previous role, I knew a chap who was an uber coffee nerd, in the most positive way! He was the guy people loved to associate with. I went back to the Costa Coffee franchise and told them I had this guy who I wanted to bring in because he could spread the coffee love and create the right culture. They declined, but I did it anyway. It was a calculated risk. I was unleashing my inner CEO, and it turned out to be the right decision.

I brought him in, and he created belief, energy and passion among all the baristas in the stores. It went beyond making the perfect cup of coffee and into latte art, texture and coffee blending. Our baristas became so passionate about the work that I sent them to local barista competitions. No other coffee chain in Singapore did that at the time. It wasn't always about the chain or the brand; it demonstrated that we were fundamentally committed to coffee quality and the love for what we did. That passion was infectious, and our launch was hugely successful; the brand continues to grow.

Jeremy

As a westerner living and working in Singapore for more than 20 years, did you discern the culture differences with regard to driving ownership through the organisation?

Steen

I did screw up a couple of times through being too 'western' in my approach early on in my time in Asia. I failed fast and failed hard! But I also learned how to do things early on, to the extent that I now say I am culture-blind when it comes to the East and West. I've worked in 40 countries and have spent time getting to understand people's character, rather than making an assumption based on their origin.

There are certain tactics I find useful for Asia, such as the need to be more succinct and not ramble on as some leaders in western organisations do. Make sure you are understood and allow time for them to upskill. The reason why it worked well with 4Fingers Crispy Chicken and Costa Coffee was that I made sure they understood exactly what was needed to be successful.

Some people get a little lost but with the right support they eventually get out of their comfort zone and move forward. If you can look beyond culture and see the enlightenment in people, feel their confidence and their willingness to act, you know the rest is about learning, failing and achieving. You also need the infrastructure to strengthen and support their personal growth, which in turn grows your business.

I lived this ethos when I led 4Fingers, and it worked; we overcame one of the biggest industry pain points. In food and beverage businesses across Asia, the typical employee turnover rate is between 70% and 100%. Nearly all your staff would leave within 12 months. By scrapping the usual ways of working, by empowering our mini-CEOs and unleashing talent at all levels, we reduced it to less than 25% turnover across our key worker population. In parallel, we had zero turnover in our management team, which demonstrates the success of an empowering culture.

Understanding food and beverage financials helped in this respect. Attrition is one of the highest avoidable costs; there are the [expenses of] rehiring, training and overstaffing. It's about 10% of payroll costs. To support the culture, I use the costs of attrition to create a budget for salary increases and loyalty bonuses, to reward the people who consistently contribute. It creates a positive buzz and reduces the cost of attrition. The longer people stay, the more productive they are, which means a more consistent experience and service for customers. This creates profitability earlier than in the usual cycle.

We look after our staff, and our staff look after our business. It's very much like the Disney approach of first taking care of your staff, and the rest takes care of itself.

Jeremy

And a big part of 'the rest' is, of course, your customers. How did they buy into the 4Fingers philosophy?

Steen

It's about creating a brand. The brand for me is the best way to create value because people say, "I'll pay more for that because it is brand ABC." What we saw was that when people talked about 4Fingers the level of engagement, not just with the food but with the brand, was mind-blowing. When I left, I told my team that my mission was accomplished. It was to build a great and exciting brand, and we had achieved it.

'Brand' won when we hit 100,000 followers on Facebook, and there were 5,000 people who not only liked but also posted to engage with the brand. We touched people's hearts, not only their minds, at mealtimes. Our brand approach was to be the equivalent of what Red Bull is to Coca-Cola: a carbonated soft drink compared to another carbonated soft drink, but a cooler, more subversive brand. I said, "I'm going to be cooler when compared to KFC and other QSR [quick service restaurant] companies." The secret sauce was not on our chicken; it was in our staff.

Jeremy

From these amazing experiences as CEO, investor and entrepreneur, what advice would you give leaders about unleashing their inner CEOs and driving new levels of success?

Steen

The first thing is to be crystal clear about your destination, because without a destination you will never arrive.

The second thing is to understand the culture of the business and how empowered, or otherwise, your people feel, in readiness to buy into the vision of unleashing their inner CEO.

There is no one-size-fits-all solution, which is why the initial analysis is so important; the leadership team can make informed decisions, rather than try to impose a feeling, a directive or a will.

The third element would be to quickly get the buy-in from your management team, who will be responsible for making it happen. Be clear about the vision and what the business is trying to achieve and how you shape targets, style and co-working, to ensure consistency and alignment as you implement. And as a leader, getting buy-in from your team is essential. A leader without followers is just a guy walking.

I have seen this approach work. I'd wager there would be increases in shareholder value, employer brand value, employee and customer satisfaction for companies that unleash their inner CEOs.

"I really believed in bothering my mini-CEOs as little as possible, once they knew the direction and what was expected. That way, it was easy to spot who stepped up."

Steen Puggaard

CHAPTER 4:

Supercharging Organisational Progress

Introduction

The previous chapter covered the leadership mindset and culture of the organisation. These must be set up so that the business is ready to shift in structural terms, flattening hierarchies and enabling personnel to unleash their inner CEO. This, in turn, will drive an *organisational* shift. And this transformation is the first of two key components which are critical for unleashing human potential in this new era for businesses everywhere.

The second component is the *personal* shift; this will enable each person, at any level within the workforce, to unleash their inner CEO to thrive and perform in this new era. These two components must be in place to create a stable and strong foundation in preparation for the pillars you build upon it.

The organisational component is the bedrock, and we will cover it in detail throughout this chapter, which will be of particular interest to those responsible for implementing the cultural and operational changes – leaders, HR professionals and line managers, among others.

An effective support system can measure and evolve the activity. The whole process is underpinned by the executive leadership team getting it right first. If they don't – and this is key – it will fail. Only when the foundation structure has been secured can HR and line managers identify the likely in-role CEOs, assess them and define what is needed from them. At that point, implementation can begin.

This starts with an assessment to identify individuals' strengths and gaps across the required knowledge, skills and behaviours in my Empowered Leadership Model, the 4Es: Envision, Engage, Execute and Excel (see Chapter 5). The output will be a targeted development plan to build on existing strengths, close gaps and nurture new leadership and management skill sets that will be required as they evolve their in-role CEO abilities.

They can develop these skills through what I call the 'development mosaic', which provides several different activities that an in-role CEO and their line manager can own to drive the development of their skills and values. Their line manager and HR play a pivotal role at this stage, working with them on a road map to support their first 90 days as they unleash their inner CEO.

The foundation stone relating to 'organisation', covered throughout this chapter, incorporates the support infrastructure to collaborate, guide and work with the unleashed population. Then it is about getting the 'personal shift' correctly positioned so that your people can do things in the right way from the start. We will cover that in the next chapter.

The Organisation

Successfully transforming the organisation has to start by decentralising authority. An article by William Craig[31] in *Forbes* magazine in February 2018 explained that a flat organisation cuts through some of the clutter of hierarchical responsibility and project ownership, so it becomes localised within your teams. And those teams, in turn, have greater autonomy to collaborate and make decisions that directly affect the daily operations without consulting higher leaders. Furthermore, they can try out new ideas and engage in innovative thinking regularly.

Great examples are companies like Zappos, Gumroad and Medium.com, as covered by William Craig's article. His parting words resonate for all organisations looking to empower in-role CEOs:

> At the end of the day, though, the idea to come back to is that the people who perform the most important work within your organisation should be doing more of the thinking about how your company will meet its future success. It helps them feel more engaged in their careers – and it also takes some of the decision-making burden off your managers. Innovation doesn't just happen at the CEO or upper-management levels, after all. It can happen anywhere, but it takes the right kind of leadership to foster it.

Decentralising authority means you need to think about the structure of your organisation. It is important to consider whether it is ready to facilitate leadership at all levels. Have you got too many levels of hierarchy? How do you break down traditional hierarchies? How do you flatten the structures? How do you drive a culture of empowerment and the mentality of ownership, right through the organisation?

Once you've established the most suitable leadership mindset for your company, you'll find that organisational culture can more easily evolve to unlock progress. Because if you don't have a culture that is embracing and accepting of this new process (each person taking ownership and leading at their level), this will negatively impact the entire business and your structure will quickly fizzle out. Therefore, organisational culture evolution is the absolute key. To enable it further, as we covered in Chapter 1, we have to transform digitally. *Digital* technology enables greater levels of empowerment and ownership.

Smarp, the employee engagement technology solutions company, explained that almost half of mid-market firms believe that digital transformation is key to employee empowerment.[32]

This means giving everyone the right tools and tech so they can collaborate, communicate and take ownership of these things, and do it quickly. Therefore, the leadership, culture and digital elements need to be in place from a mentality shift point of view, as well as a structural point of view.

Once this is established, the ownership for operationalising the new structure and approach must sit across two traditional functions. The first is organisational development and design (OD), which as a function looks at the ongoing structure of the organisation and how it works, and then at how managers and teams step up, implement and action the new way forward. This has to be led by the second function, HR. If you get this right, you will unleash the in-role CEOs across your organisation. You will support them with the right tools, line management support, learning and training to help them transcend their job role and contribute more broadly to the organisation's operational and strategic imperatives.

As you flatten the structure and provide leadership at all levels, there are definite pros, but there are cons too. Flattening the structure comes with many benefits because you're developing ownership for the business within each role throughout the organisation. But – and here comes one of the major cons – if I am someone who has unleashed their inner CEO, and I look at the organisation and see a flattened hierarchy, I won't see many levels above me, and I can't see a defined career path.

Therefore, any organisation committed to unleashing their inner CEOs and sponsoring leadership at all levels must think through how to recognise and reward new behaviours, emerging skills and those making an impact beyond their job role, as they contribute to broader business health. Having a thought-through recognition approach will help to minimise our 'con' above and place a value on the organisational change desired. This will ensure those stepping up are rewarded and satisfied in-role, as they develop and grow. For many this will represent an ideal situation, as they no longer feel the pressure or need to be promoted, while having the ability to contribute into the longer term at their level, in their role, to the broader strategic aims of the business. This may solve generational issues and long-termer fatigue, and may ultimately be a more inclusive and valued policy.

Below are some of the tactics to consider as the organisation formalises its recognition and reward approach. This should be the starting point and will spark additional ideas suited to the organisation and individuals concerned.

Figure 3: Recognition and Reward Suggestions

Ideas and suggestions		
Recognition	Non-monetary reward	Monetary rewards
Senior leadership team meeting presentation	Time off for wellness and personal pampering	Bonus based on qualitative and quantitative impact on the business and other stakeholders (rewarding both behaviours and results)
Certification system (bronze, silver and gold in-role CEOs) based on specific measurable and provable criteria that all those unleashing their inner CEO can aspire to	Party or awards event for the individual and their team or collaborative group	Annual increases in salary, on top of normal increase, possible up to an incremental percentage defined by the business (such as an additional 5% based on in-role CEO performance)
Gamify the unleashing of the inner CEOs: award badges and merits linked to non-monetary awards	Paid dinner for the individual with friends, partner or family	Bonus payment on attaining bronze, silver, gold certification as in-role CEO
Appointing an executive leader mentor to accompany the journey for specific projects or points in time	Paid holiday for the individual and their family or partner	Line manager discretionary budget to provide relatively small monetary bonuses during regular reviews throughout the year
Inclusion in relevant strategic meetings	Learning and development to grow strategic and leadership skills (outside normal learning path)	CEO Special Award – a competition in parallel with other activities to identify and reward the best new initiative that has biggest impact on the business, on people and on the customer: a large one-off cash prize and public recognition
Lifestyle awards linked to merits and badges collected	Trips and visits to other parts of the company (globally) to share best practices and experiences	New contract, extended contract or long-term contract for those independent freelance workers contributing with consistency and excellence to the business

Having all this in place, upfront, enables people to feel empowered to take ownership and to be rewarded and recognised, so they develop from within, rather than by traditional routes.

Getting to this point means you have OD owning the new structure, and new ways of working in the business. You've also got human talent leaders, HR and others communicating what's going to happen and upskilling everybody involved, so they're owning and correctly enabling this culture of empowerment. Because, if support, training and coaching is approached in the same way as it would be for individuals' core job roles, it's not going to work. Therefore, organisational development and training must also evolve.

The organisational pillars need to be in place to secure this solid foundation. Clarity of expectations and a clear progression pathway, like that provided by this book, are needed. If they aren't in place, progress will quickly fizzle out. The other side of this is that when people are given scope and a structure for creativity and innovation, the evidence suggests that empowering leadership is more likely to be effective:

> ...empowering leaders are much more effective at influencing employee creativity and citizenship behavior (i.e., behavior that is not formally recognized or rewarded like helping co-workers or attending work functions that aren't mandatory) than routine task performance.

This is from a useful research summary from the *Harvard Business Review* which goes deeper into this point: ('When empowering employees works and when it doesn't').[33]

As well as processes and skills for the people who are unleashing their inner CEO, you'll need to empower the existing line managers. You need to equip them with new skills to support these newly unleashed leaders. They need to learn how to support, how to develop, and how to provide the unleashed leaders with management and leadership insight.

> The trend for this has already been happening because over the past five years organisations have been seeking ways to get more from their employees. Organisations have been downsizing, and there has been more pressure applied to individuals to step up and beyond their operational role. There is also evidence to suggest that unleashing inner CEOs has occurred by accident, as a lever to push the performance and grow the organisation at a time of fundamental shift and transformation. That said, it has not always been formalised, supported or recognised in KPI and reward terms.

In an article published in *Personnel Today* in September 2016, 'Why it is crucial to create leaders at all levels',[34] Dr Tim Sparkes wrote:

> A poll conducted on behalf of Saba found that nearly 70% of employed US adults consider themselves leaders, regardless of their job title. There's a growing sense that people are itching to lead irrespective of whether it comes with a traditional leadership name tag. Younger generations are more expectant. You give them the opportunity first, then they prove their worth. The workplace is shapeshifting too rapidly for people to sit patiently and earn their stripes.

If we consider the millennial mindset, they're ready for this. They are poised to take on responsibility and use their initiative. They are ready, willing and able. So, there are leaders who are ready to go. Organisations haven't been attracting enough of the right people because they haven't been systematic in their approach. Tim Sparkes' article demonstrates the shift from a traditional hierarchical structure. There's a readiness, a willingness and an ability, as long as it's supported. This shows that the time is right to unleash inner CEOs around the world and in every walk of life. The full potential of the next generation of leaders is, as yet, untapped and unrealised.

At the same time, it's vital to recognise that many prospective leaders may not identify themselves as leaders. If the organisation is short on diversity in its senior leadership team, others may not see themselves reflected at that level. So, HR and managers have a part to play in identifying potential and building confidence. Once a process of unleashing leaders at all levels has begun, it can accelerate an organisation's diversity, equity and inclusion strategy, by creating increased opportunities across the organisation for development and growth. This in turn influences a company's culture and brand, with the potential to attract new diverse talent. So, it's essential that line managers are supported by effective diversity, equity and inclusion training and best practice, to ensure that factors such as unconscious bias do not adversely filter the processes for identifying and unleashing leadership at all levels.

More evidence that organic change is already under way can be found in an article by Mark van den Boogaart, the principal consultant at Executive Central, published in June 2019. In 'Five tips to empower leaders at all levels of your organisation',[35] he writes, "Make leadership an activity rather than a title in your organisation."

Again, this points to a mindset shift that employees are already making. It's time for the traditional hierarchy to catch up. The caveat is that while the title may not be awarded yet, supporting infrastructure for recognition and reward must be. It is central to employee satisfaction and a feeling of inclusion and belonging, and something that I've noticed in my work with organisations to be increasingly rare.

In this book, I aim to give leaders and their people – whether employees, independent workers, or their future workforce – the vision and the tools to unleash their inner CEOs. It's an exciting time for the future of work.

Implications for Management

There are two key component actions for the organisation's line management: first, to make sure everyone still performs in their core role; and second, to be the enablers behind those unleashing their inner CEO. This often requires competency frameworks or talent management processes. These need to be refreshed to identify what these capabilities are in terms of knowledge, skills and behaviours. For those who are willing to step up, an assessment framework needs to be in place to ascertain their suitability and competence, and to identify their strengths and skill gaps. This, in turn, becomes a powerful line management tool to mix a core job developmental focus with an increased focus on the new, more strategic knowledge, skills and behaviours we want our in-role CEOs to embrace and develop.

When leaders at all levels are identified, these unique support structures can be put in place for the individuals to create a development plan. The line managers for those stepping up to become in-role CEOs will become the conduit between the action and the impact of the action on others, the business and the growth of the individual.

The first six months will require feedback loops and coaching to facilitate close support for those unleashing their inner CEO. The organisational level needs a structured reporting process that accurately measures the improvement and ongoing strengths and gaps of our unleashed population as they evolve into their roles.

The structure becomes a fluid personal development plan that is owned at the organisational level by HR, then driven through the line manager, while ultimately being owned by in-role CEOs themselves, so they are working on building the skills they need to demonstrate leadership and management capabilities. This will be central to how they will be measured, how they will be recognised and rewarded for their new role, and what it means for their potential career path. And that career path could be within the job role or a part of a fast-tracked leadership pipeline journey. It very much depends on the person, their motivations and their stretch.

It has been observed that when people take ownership of this expanded role, there is a great benefit to the wellbeing of employees. Following a two-year study of 20,000 employees, conducted at Birmingham University Business School (UK), Dr Daniel Wheatley stated:

"Greater levels of control over work tasks have the potential to generate significant benefits for the employee, which was found to be evident in the levels of reported wellbeing. The positive effects associated with informal flexibility and working at home, offer further support to the suggestion that schedule control is highly valued and important to employees 'enjoying' work."[36]

We see evidence of companies that have removed traditional hierarchies and micromanagement operations: WL Gore (Gore-Tex), WordPress[37] and Google.[38] Tony Hsieh, the CEO of Zappos, pushed 'flat' to a whole new level, adopting 'holacracy' principles.[39] This is essentially the practice of self-management, which is one of the latest trends evolving for governance within flatter hierarchies. These are customisable self-management practices where roles are defined around work, authority is distributed and the organisation is regularly updated in small iterations.

The jury is out as to whether the holacracy model is truly workable as a long-term approach – it is clear that there have been mixed experiences – but it is refreshing to see experimentation happening at this level.

Case Study: Exploring a Flatter Organisational Culture – Nike

Nike is a 20th century business which has evolved its workplace and workforce management through a flat structure, and completely shifted its culture as an organisation. Nike has embraced the flatter structure by taking out multiple layers of management. Nike embraced, lived and breathed ways to empower individuals and small collaborative groups, either working in the same function or on different projects to find breakthrough ways forward to unleash innovation at all levels.[40]

One of the main benefits of this structure is that it creates room for decision-making to happen without ideas getting trapped in a traditional, bureaucratic chain of command. On average, it takes a year and a half to launch a project at Nike, from initial design to the actual crafting of products. This level of agility also gives Nike teams the ability to keep their ear to the ground when it comes to trends and customer preferences and make changes as they see fit.

Another plus of Nike's flat structure is that it facilitates transparency in all markets. Managers are responsible for small teams and decisions happen faster, with more collaboration between individual parties. Nike's smaller regional teams typically respond more to customer demand and distribution needs, while overall factory orders remain within the authority of Nike's headquarters.

Annually, Nike's products undergo approximately 30,000 to 40,000 developments: cosmetic changes, colour updates and new features occur regularly. Nike's branches typically focus on apparel, while footwear remains largely in the realm of global headquarters. The independence of Nike subsidiaries and regional subsets, and their singular focus, allows for these changes to happen continually without interference from governing bodies or deviation from Nike's overall brand.

This is a call to those companies that are still struggling with the 20th century model, inviting them to evolve into a 21st century model rapidly. Because if they don't, the organisation will always be controlled by corporate headquarters and is likely to remain locked into hierarchical decision-making. Nike has demonstrated that a big company that was geared for success in the last century can change, shift its culture, become more agile, and drive empowerment to levels that have not been seen before in so large a company.

While there are significant benefits to flattening the structure, we do also need to acknowledge there are potential downsides to consider. Naturally, each organisation will be different. You'll have to consider the disadvantages and have plans in place, along with robust rules for moving forward.

US-based Southwest Airlines has continually empowered and engaged its employees in new ways.[41] It had a mentality shift and a culture shift that flipped the traditional view of what its priorities were as an organisation, in terms of fulfilling the wishes of shareholders. It has positioned its priorities in this new order: employees, then customers, then shareholders. Happy and engaged employees will always treat customers well – which in turn will encourage customers to come back – and they'll be more motivated. This will lead to better performance and will continue to impact customer satisfaction, and of course, the business, which will keep shareholders happy. Southwest Airlines proactively encourages its employees to unleash their inner CEO and take responsibility for the company as a whole, not just their specific role.

A recent *Harvard Business Review* article makes a comparison between eastern and western practices.[42] The authors found there was little to no difference between eastern and western companies when greater levels of empowerment were driven through the business. Some companies in Asia have gone beyond the traditional, politically run companies and have embraced entrepreneurship and enterprise. They're driving rapid growth by flattening structures in their organisation.

A Vietnamese dairy company, Vinamilk, talks of two key empowerment points: know who to identify as potential leaders at their level and then how to best empower them without overburdening them. ASQ published some interesting points about how employee empowerment works:[43]

"Job enlargement: Changing the scope of the job to include a greater portion of the horizontal process.

Example: A bank teller not only handles deposits and disbursement but also distributes traveler's checks and sells certificates of deposit.

Job enrichment: Increasing the depth of the job to include responsibilities that have traditionally been carried out at higher levels of the organization.

Example: The teller also has the authority to help a client fill out a loan application, and to determine whether or not to… approve the loan.

Employee empowerment also means… giving up some of the power traditionally held by management, which means managers also must take on new roles, knowledge, and responsibilities."

For organisational leadership to move forward, leaders need to identify who will be able to step up in the organisation and truly unleash their inner CEO to become a bona fide in-role CEO.

What Next?

In the next chapter, following another interview – this time with human capital and talent professional Emma Saxby – I'll guide you through the *personal* component, which builds on the *organisational* foundation.

Emma's interview acts as a convenient bridge between the organisational and the personal. Her theme and passion is all about unlocking the power within our employee population. To do this, we have to have the organisational conditions and structures in place, before we then empower our people to step up and achieve great things, as leaders at all levels.

INTERVIEW WITH
EMMA SAXBY

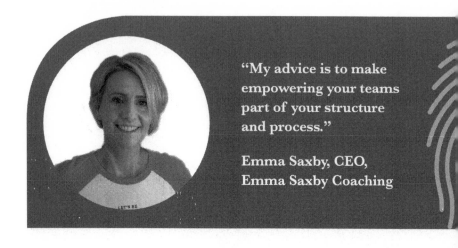

"My advice is to make empowering your teams part of your structure and process."

Emma Saxby, CEO,
Emma Saxby Coaching

Emma Saxby has spent the last 12 years in the world of HR, in various roles. She started in learning and development, moved into talent management, and then focused on senior-level executive development, leadership pipeline and graduate development. Emma has worked for large multinationals such as AXA Insurance and DSM, the purpose-led sciences company. She recently founded her own coaching business, operating across Asia Pacific, UK and Europe.

In this interview, she emphasises the centrality of trust and how this must be championed at all levels of the organisation, including HR. She puts line management under the spotlight, pointing to how it must shift from a traditional supervisory role into one of empowerment, and how cross-functional and multi-project work can enable new possibilities.

Jeremy

In the spirit of this book, as we consider how businesses will evolve over the next decade, why is it important to have leaders at all levels in the organisation?

Emma

It's important because the environment has changed so much. With a much faster-paced market, even in the more secure corporate markets, things are changing and evolving. Younger people coming into the business are wanting to move into flexible roles, achieve high standards at high levels and grow themselves as business professionals.

Organisations everywhere are breaking down traditional hierarchies. Multinationals operate in different time zones, in different ways, across cultures, at differing experience levels and with office-based as well as remote teams. It's multidimensional and requires new thinking around how to unleash every person's capability to the max.

As a result, because the world is changing, companies need to keep up. If we just stick with what we've always done, we'll get what we always got. The way to change the game is to unleash the inner CEOs of our people – at all levels.

It's fundamentally important to have empowered people at every level because, primarily, it increases engagement and productivity. You get people's buy-in and value. People are so transient now that if you don't get that buy-in, you don't get the value and you lose people rather than unleashing their power, so they stay engaged.

Jeremy

What impact can companies expect if they unleash the inner CEOs at every level in their organisations?

Emma

It's all in the results. If you don't have people striving to achieve the next thing, you're not going to meet the targets you set and you're not going to stay with or ahead of your competition. You're going to lose shareholders' and stakeholders' interest. Many companies nowadays are being forced into mass restructuring because they have to adapt. Whereas if they had put a bit more forethought into it and had leaders who were enlightened and mentally ready, it would have accelerated transformation and reduced the need for continual short-term restructure attempts. In this scenario, they lose sight of the long term and slip into 'old ways' of leading, managing and supervising. It doesn't encourage empowerment or employee engagement, which is risky in today's VUCA [volatile, uncertain, complex and ambiguous] environment.

Jeremy

In the companies you have worked for, how have the more enlightened leaders created the conditions, climate and environment that unleash our inner CEOs?

Emma

There are two things that stand out. One of them is culture: company culture, built on a platform of trust. Because to empower people, you need to trust them. The more enlightened leaders I have worked with have one thing in common: they have released their egos. They've opened up to the fact that other people can bring those leadership skills to their roles and contribute to the organisation. I'm fortunate to have worked with several forward-thinking leaders. They can unleash their people's inner CEOs, and they trust them to own it.

The second thing they do is invest. They invest in the younger generation to accelerate their development and allow them to contribute, beyond their job role, early in their career. This is motivating and engaging for new, young employees. They also invest in upskilling the rest of their organisational population, which helps to introduce the desired cultural shifts and environment so that everyone feels they can contribute strategically and operationally to the business. In my experience, the companies that do this well have a strong link between company leadership and human resources leadership.

Jeremy

For some companies, there is a lot of trial and error. How relevant is the mantra of failing fast, often and early for these transforming companies?

Emma

Very! It doesn't necessarily mean you're going to be successful immediately, but we do see evidence of early success in some of these businesses. It's because they create a space and an environment where people can test, feel empowered and upskill simultaneously. Failing fast, failing early and learning from it is precisely what they do.

A solid platform of trust must underpin this. I've experienced it when it is not lived and breathed as a belief but implemented as more of a marketing exercise. "This is what we want to do. Here's this beautiful-looking culture. Here's what we say."

Unfortunately, in some companies, the leaders don't model behaviours. HR does not own its message, and no one champions the cause. Therefore, it becomes too risky for individual contributors to step up, experiment, fail, learn and take greater ownership. A lack of trust builds and fear of failure prevails.

So, it's critical for leaders at all levels to take decisive action and unleash their inner CEOs. They support the process through upskilling, removing layers of management and creating more of a coaching culture to support the shift. They also examine the company structure and make bold moves to change the traditional ways of working. They embrace the new, for example, remote working, flexible hours, workplace changes, and more collaborative workspaces with new policies, rules of the road and processes that support the shifts, rather than hindering progress.

Jeremy

You mentioned removing layers in the business. So, as we unleash our inner CEOs and witness broader ownership at all levels in the business, what is the role of the line managers and how do you mobilise and engage them in managing differently?

Emma

This is the most crucial part. Just imagine what you can achieve when you have a team that feels empowered and self-driven. They'll be the ones who propel the business to new heights. When it comes to people managers, you have to deconstruct their traditional role and make them enablers of a truly empowered organisation, where their teams feel safe to take ownership and contribute beyond their job role.

If I had a magic wand, I'd repurpose 80% of line managers and upskill the remainder to be coaches, guides and collaborators for growth. By accelerating and supporting leadership at all levels, you grow people to grow the organisation.

This needs to become a part of the company's DNA. It's a cultural shift underpinned by new values that accelerate the ability to take ownership at every level in the organisation, supported by amazing coaches who become the catalysts for unleashing the inner CEOs of our best and brightest. My advice is to make empowering your teams part of your structure and process. This is as much about organisational design as it is about how we do things.

The company has to be structured correctly first, creating an environment where people flourish. Then managers don't feel threatened by the continuing, traditional focus on short-term results and overprocessed supervisory activity, such as performance management administration and so on. They will need to be repurposed and reskilled, and by doing this, you will engage a hugely important part of the population who will be the fuel behind unleashing the inner CEOs.

Jeremy

How does this manifest itself in how work gets done as we move into a truly empowered state of unleashed inner CEOs and repurposed line managers?

Emma

In my experience, it accelerates companies becoming more project-focused, led by cross-functional teams who are empowered to own the objective and work together for successful implementation. In my last role, I was genuinely empowered to contribute beyond my job role and was taking part in over 10 different projects. I was even leading a couple of bigger ones.

Interestingly, it almost becomes the job role, and you find you are operating at different levels in each project. This helps to take out traditional hierarchies and work differently as self-directed teams. I was an individual contributor to some projects and with a leading or managing role for others. Many organisations are moving in that direction now, to the extent that HR no longer forces static job descriptions but makes the whole approach more fluid, so job role, function and the expected broader contribution to the business are recognised. I ended up doing 10% of the work based on my traditional job description but was able to contribute more to the company, across a broader remit and with higher performance, because I embraced and owned it, as did many of my colleagues. I think that is the essence of embodying your unleashed inner CEO.

Jeremy

This transcends the traditional way in which many companies allocate roles and create boxes to contain specific job descriptions, doesn't it?

Emma

Yes, absolutely. Rather than pigeon-holing our people, we see a holistic, longer-term contribution. This transcends roles and takes people down a path they can grow on, by being involved in different projects, across many parts of the business, rather than being locked into one linear route and role. It's far more motivating and ultimately a more productive way of working.

Jeremy

In terms of the broader implications for organisations on this trajectory, how does it impact the way we should attract, recruit, develop, retain and grow an increasingly valuable human capital pool?

Emma

As an HR professional, I'd say, "You can come into this organisation. We will invest our time and energy in developing you, but we're also going to strengthen your strengths, and give you flexibility around the things that you need to be able to contribute, far beyond your job role."

It's all about having a much more flexible approach to HR and human capital management. Having more of a pick-and-mix mentality as far as the roles and benefits you're offering, so it meets people's individual needs, not a collective fit-all-into-a-certain-box approach. A lot of companies use this more dynamic approach to attract talent and do a great job of attraction and recruitment. But they don't follow through by delivering on their promises, and it doesn't take long for people to react. "Whoa, this is not at all what you sold me. This is what we discussed, and this is nowhere near where we are."

I've seen that so many times, and then people leave. So, if you're going to create an environment that embraces a flexible, new way to deal with human resources, you have to believe it and you have to systematically deliver on your promises. Then you'll have the right people in your organisation because it's attractive. It's more empowering for the organisation and for the individuals.

Jeremy

If an organisation goes down this road but they don't execute well and it fizzles out, what is the higher cost?

Emma

The cost can be huge actually, as it relates to engagement: how engaged or otherwise our employees, at all levels, are, as contributors to the company.

As I mentioned earlier, you'll lose people to competitors who are doing it well. You'll find it harder to attract new talent as your employer branding reputation will suffer and, in the digital world, that can quickly go viral. As an organisation, you wouldn't grow, and you wouldn't evolve. So that then impacts the business – you lose people, you lose skills, you lose the ability to grow the business, and ultimately this can lead to total failure. This is being evidenced now; the failure rate of companies is at its highest in a century.

Jeremy

You talked about the need for a new DNA for what makes up the profile of organisations with high-contributing employees. What are the key components that make up this unique DNA?

Emma

Some of the words that come to mind when I picture organisational DNA are trust, courage, creativity, flexibility, success-minded, ownership and recognition.

Trust is the foundation because everyone should feel safe, be allowed to be open and feel supported. Then individuals will often need to unlock their courage in trying something new.

I say creativity as we have to unlock an innovative mindset of what is possible at all levels. New ideas can come from anywhere, not only from the top. We all have to be more flexible as the environments we work in are increasingly uncertain. We may have to adapt our business model, try new things and work in different ways. Everyone needs to be on board with that.

We have to be success-minded and keep our eyes on the prize, particularly if we are involved in multiple projects. And to do this we have to take ownership, not just in our job role but as part of collaborative teams working on projects impacting the whole business.

If everyone embodies this new DNA, you are unleashing the inner CEOs within your company and success is inevitable.

The final piece is recognition. If people are changing, willing to make mistakes and to learn from them, work differently and drive greater success, it is essential also to recognise and reward these new behaviours. This will build momentum and demonstrate the value the company is putting on those who model the new DNA by unleashing their inner CEOs.

Jeremy

If I asked you to advise a company on how to unleash their inner CEOs, where would you start?

Emma

It begins with a culture that supports the new DNA. I would ask questions around that. What does the culture look and feel like? What is it that they want it to be? What are the foundations? Then we'd look at the gaps. Once the gaps are filled, it's about the support infrastructure to get people quickly up to speed, which is a crucial success factor. What are the desired values, the new knowledge, skills and behaviours that will drive success? Companies have to get in front of this and invest in the change they want. Otherwise, it simply won't happen. You can't force-fit new thinking into an existing, outdated model. It requires a shift in mentality and how you do things.

Do it well and do it fast, and that will be a competitive advantage all around.

Jeremy

Yes, so it needs the right leadership to champion the cause and be the catalysts for sustainable change.

Emma

Yes, it does, and it also models what great leadership looks like for those individuals unleashing their inner CEO. There's an exercise I've done many times in training sessions. You ask people, "What is it that you admired, or what is it that you loved about a leader who had an impact on you?" I love listening to the answers. You get the most beautiful responses from people: real, raw responses, and that's what I see as 'self-leadership'.

It's the things they admire that help them to develop and strive to be better than they are, that challenge them, and help them get comfortable with being uncomfortable. That's them starting their journey to unleash their leadership, their inner CEO.

When you do this exercise in a business where the leadership team is highly valued, you'll typically get a list of top traits, behaviours and actions the participants can model. Self-leadership is what they do after the session and is a great way to measure success for the newly empowered organisation.

Jeremy

What would you put in place to build momentum and continue to support the people who are taking ownership to unleash their inner CEOs?

Emma

I'd set up a buddy system in parallel with the supporting elements we have covered. We did this in one of my previous organisations, and it worked well. Peer support is something that is often missed but is helpful when you have a flatter, more interdependent, collaborative culture.

Whether you're an executive, a CEO or a graduate, you pair up with a buddy. That person becomes somebody who supports you, helps you practise for meetings or presentations, and is someone to work with as mutual coaching support.

When we ask people to be courageous and take bold new steps, make mistakes and learn from them, doubt is bound to creep in. This buddy system supports you, more informally than your line manager, but as an additional resource.

"If we just stick with what we've always done, we'll get what we've always got. The way to change the game is to unleash the inner CEOs of our people – at all levels."

Emma Saxby

CHAPTER 5:

Making It Happen: Unleashing Leadership at All Levels

Introduction

In the previous chapter, we covered the *organisational* component of unleashing the inner CEO. Now we'll proceed to what needs to be in place at a *personal* level. In other words, at the human talent level where HR professionals and managers are working with individual contributors to unleash their inner CEOs.

The personal side of organisational development must support workers to unleash their inner CEO. It's an opportunity for people to prove their abilities and become leaders at their current level as they do remarkable work and make their contribution. Individuals need to have a framework for focusing on the development of the knowledge, skills and behaviours that make the difference. This is where the 4Es Empowered Leadership Model (see Chapter 2) becomes practical. An empowered organisation, with members of the workforce unleashed as in-role CEOs, has a massive impact on results. An excellent example of this is given by Ed Evans, executive vice-president and chief HR officer at Four Seasons, who attributes the company's success to its employees and culture, as summarised in an article published in *Forbes* magazine in February 2019, 'Leaders Can Cultivate True Employee Empowerment'.[44]

"The same level of care that we extend to our guests applies to our people. By empowering our employees and giving them the tools and trust needed to succeed, they, in turn, carry our values forward, connecting deeply with our guests and creating the memorable experiences that Four Seasons is known for."

Ed Evans, executive vice-president and chief HR officer, Four Seasons

Throughout the organisation, there's a level of empowerment where people are stepping up. This inside-out approach creates employee and customer satisfaction. Everybody wins. As workforces evolve over the next five to 10 years, they will become more digitally enabled and increasingly remote, which will result in the blended workforces we've referred to throughout the book.

With this in mind, it's clear that unleashing the inner CEO throughout organisations is not merely a 'nice-to-have'. It's a must-do for future development. Otherwise, companies, their leaders and their workforce will be left behind. We need leaders at all levels regardless of where they are, who they are, where they operate, how they're employed and how they choose to use relevant tools. This demonstrates a solid case for getting it right and treating all employees – regardless of whether they are permanent workers or non-permanent contractors – in a similar way, which will provide a sense of empowerment, purpose and belonging to propel them forward.

To recap Chapter 2, there are four key areas in the process for robust identification and support of candidates who are ready to embrace the opportunity to become an in-role CEO:

- An empowering, supportive organisation and management structure

- Assessment of potential candidates

- A 90-day fast-start, measurable road map and development planner

- A way to recognise and reward performance for those unleashing their inner CEO and making progress

From a personal perspective, you must be practical about what needs to be in place. First, it's important for those stepping up to be willing and able to take ownership of their development.

Also, guidelines need to be in place for building skills and assessing and tracking progress to evolve personal development plans, as candidates embrace the new vision and develop their leadership and management capabilities. What's required is a development plan to take your people forward for at least the first 90 days.

Those willing to go on this journey need to be ready and able to develop a network of peer and management level contacts as a support infrastructure while growing in this role. These two things go hand in hand.

Everyone has the potential to unleash their inner CEO, but the reality is that there will be people who stand out, and from there, others may be inspired to step up.

Who Are the Right Candidates?

For an individual contributor, a key question is: are you going to embrace leadership at your level? Also, how can you grow in the role, and how can you become a leader, be rewarded and grow yourself, rather than following the traditional path of promotion to move forward?

For HR professionals and line managers, the question becomes: how do you identify the right people in order to help them unleash their inner CEO?

It is true to say that everyone has the potential and opportunity to step up, but not all will do so. So, to make the process more efficient, some groundwork can be done to ensure the process includes individuals who have the will and aptitude to succeed.

As a starting point, the ideal candidates will stand out because they will already be making an effort to achieve more than purely what's listed in their job description. They will already be stepping up when given the opportunity. Unleashing their inner CEO may not be as big a stretch for some team members as their managers may believe. Ideal candidates will already be on the journey, whether consciously or not. This is an already available power source and an opportunity to tap further potential.

My 'Five-Point Validation' star below will help provide clarity as to the qualities shown by the most promising candidates: those who have the potential to unleash their inner CEO, regardless of their organisational role or level. It is true that everyone has the potential to unleash their inner CEO, and anyone can be invited. But a human resources perspective also has to consider 'will': the attitude, willingness and readiness to get on this journey.

Figure 4: The Five-Point Validation to Identify
Potential In-Role CEO Stars

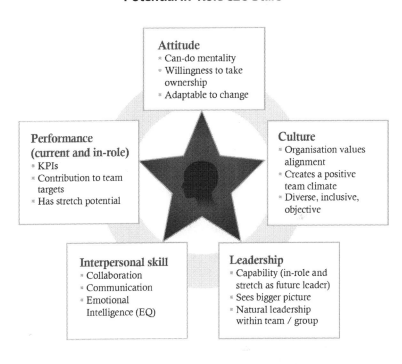

The Five-Point Validation becomes a quick checklist for managers and human capital professionals, in collaboration with individuals, to assess suitability of talent at any level to step up and unleash their inner CEO. The key validation areas are:

1. Attitude

2. Culture

3. Leadership

4. Interpersonal skill

5. Performance

The Five-Point Validation star definitions:

Attitude: a can-do mentality, willingness to take ownership and adaptability to change.

Culture: what are the organisation's values, and is this person aligned to them? What is the team culture? What are the enablers and barriers in place within the current culture, and do they need to be modified? And how does the management climate in the organisation facilitate truly unleashing and empowering people?

Leadership: this relates to capability. Are individuals demonstrating leadership capabilities in their role right now? This is about the stretch to be a future leader for the business (in hierarchical terms), or the ability to evolve within a current role and grow with it. This is also about the capacity to see the bigger picture. Also, the ability to demonstrate natural leadership in the team and group. A consideration of peer, subordinate and senior respect will be important, as this will provide support along the journey as they mobilise and encourage others in their unleashed role.

Interpersonal skill: Centred around collaboration, communication and emotional intelligence.

Performance – current and in-role: People who are demonstrating that they can perform at high levels in the organisation. Useful information can be gained from looking at individual KPIs and contributions to team (not just individual) targets, and the potential to be stretched.

Once these five validations have been understood, the discussion can be initiated. These five areas can be assessed at organisational level (for example, with HR, the line manager and another stakeholder so it is more objective rather than purely based on the subjective viewpoint of one or other inputting party). It forms the basis of an initial suitability discussion, which can also include the individual. Therefore, the components of each of the five areas must be discussed and rated objectively to initially sense check suitability. The more robust assessment comes with the 4Es assessment (introduced in Chapter 2 and explored in more depth in this chapter), which allows us to drill down and gather more meaningful feedback.

To fast-track this initial discussion, I have provided below a rating from 1–5 for each point:

- **1** indicates a lack of the right attitude or competence for the point being validated.

- **5** indicates this individual is a role model, when considering behaviour, skills, actions and results.

This simple template (and examples that follow) will support the rapid assessment of anyone in the organisation and define the most appropriate next steps.

Figure 5: Five-Point Validation Star Assessment (blank template)

Organisation Rethink – Modelling Suitability for Those Who Can Step Up as In-Role CEOs

Trait	Aspects to consider	1 = not at all > 5 = is a role model	Total
Attitude	▪ They have a can-do mentality ▪ They are willing to take ownership ▪ Adaptable to change		
Culture	▪ Organisation values alignment ▪ Creates a positive team climate ▪ Diverse, inclusive, objective		
Leadership	▪ Capability (in-role and stretch as future leader) ▪ Sees bigger picture ▪ Natural leadership within team and group		
Interpersonal skill	▪ Collaboration ▪ Communication ▪ Emotional Intelligence (EQ)		
Performance	▪ KPIs ▪ Contribution to team targets ▪ Has stretch potential		

Total Average	1,2,3 Not ready / not making progress	4,5,6 Making progress but not quite ready	7,8,9 Potential to step up with support	10,11,12 Priority two / ready with targeted support	13,14,15 Priority one stars / ready NOW

Figure 6: Example of Completed Assessment

Organisation Rethink – Modelling Suitability for Those Who
Can Step Up as In-Role CEOs

Trait	Aspects to consider	1 = not at all > 5 = is a role model	Total
Attitude	* They have a can-do mentality	4	11
	* They are willing to take ownership	3	
	* Adaptable to change	4	
Culture	* Organisation values alignment	3	7
	* Creates a positive team climate	2	
	* Diverse, inclusive, objective	2	
Leadership	* Capability (in-role and stretch as future leader)	2	6
	* Sees bigger picture	2	
	* Natural leadership within team and group	2	
Interpersonal skill	* Collaboration	3	10
	* Communication	3	
	* Emotional Intelligence (EQ)	4	
Performance	* KPIs	2	6
	* Contribution to team targets	2	
	* Has stretch potential	2	
Total Average	**8.2** (Potential to step up with support)		

> "Employees who feel their voice is heard are 4.6 times more likely to feel empowered to perform their best work. Giving them a voice and a platform is a giant leap forward in terms of empowerment and job satisfaction."[45]
>
> **Blog by SMARP titled 'Enable your employees'**

Our way of doing this is to initiate this validatory assessment, so that we go about empowering individuals in the right way, with objective and supportive stakeholders.

The Toolkit

The 4Es Empowered Leadership Assessment

The 4Es Empowered Leadership Model approach becomes the clear way to quantifiably assess skills and strengths and to identify gaps, which must naturally be followed by deciding what training, coaching and support is required to close these gaps. To underpin the importance of this, I offer an online 4Es assessment to all my customers,[46] supported by a series of vital questions to ask for each step (below), which will help facilitate coaching discussions and uncover the most appropriate support and developmental interventions to put in place. This is how to build a road map for success.

Employees or independent workers will be able to do the online assessment by themselves, but I recommend that it is also completed by a line manager. This assessment consists of a series of 36 statements around the 4Es, to understand where someone is comfortable, where they are not and what things need to be in place so they can start making changes in the right way. It then can be completed from time to time as a quantifiable measure of personal growth, impact on others and impact on the business.

The statements are closely related to the supporting key questions below, to ensure that the assessment itself is linked to the follow-up discussions, ongoing coaching and personal development. The assessment can be accessed through my website at https://performanceworks.global/theinnerceo/

For in-role CEOs, this is the way to own that development. In lieu of completing the online assessment, which I highly recommend, here are the supporting key questions that should be answered to get started. These will help fast-track immediate next steps, developmental actions and any other initial support required.

To support the person completing the assessment and their line manager, these questions then become even more relevant, moving front and centre to more consistently facilitate personal consideration, joint discussion, coaching moments and inspiration. On the back of the online assessment itself, these questions will also help bring out the reasons for certain assessment outputs and help identify strengths and development gaps. This, in turn, will lead to a more considered and personalised development plan, as part of the first 90-day journey as an in-role CEO.

These developmental questions are designed to accompany the assessment for consideration, discussion and planning, making the whole process a highly practical one. They are framed firstly for the individual to consider in terms of self-reflection, and then to discuss with their line manager.

The 4Es Empowered Leadership Model, introduced in Chapter 2, brings together the four key themes of the assessment: Envision, Engage, Execute and Excel. Figures 8–11 detail nine questions for each theme, enabling in-role CEOs and their managers to quantifiably assess progress.

Figure 7: The 4Es Empowered Leadership Model

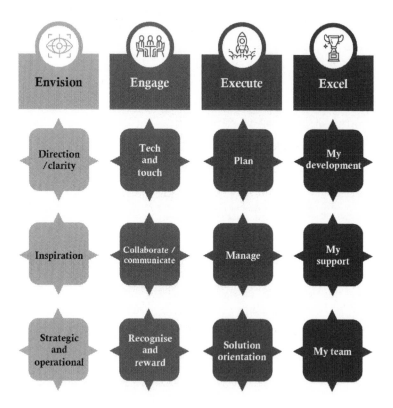

Figure 8: Questions for Envision

Envision

Own your own development – here are some critical questions you should ask yourself to get started and to reinforce your actions

Direction /clarity

- Am I clear about what I want to and can achieve outside of my job role?
- Can I clearly communicate my vision to others – including the plans and actions?
- Am I sure that my vision is SMART (specific, measurable, achievable, relevant, timebound)?

Inspiration

- How do I engage others in the journey?
- Who do I need help from to mobilise and motivate my key stakeholders?
- How do I communicate and present with impact to inspire others?

Strategic and operational

- How do I ensure my plan / actions align to the strategic aims of the organisation and my function / team?
- How do I keep in mind the big picture while implementing my action plan?
- How do I protect my own performance in my job role as well as my transition to in-role CEO?

Figure 9: Questions for Engage

Engage

Own your own development – here are some critical questions you should ask yourself to get started and to reinforce your actions

Tech and touch

- What mobile digital tools are available within my business to support internal communications and collaboration?
- What is easiest to use and implement with the maximum positive impact?
- How do I ensure quality 1-2-1 time (face-to-face or video remote) with individuals supporting / working with me?

Collaborate / communicate

- What is the formula for winning collaboration internally and externally?
- How do I enable a collaborative, high performing work group?
- What formal and informal communication needs to be in place to maximise buy in, action and impact

Recognise and reward

- How do I catch others doing it right?
- What do I expect from my line management to highlight my contribution, and help me recognise others'?
- How clear am I as to how the company will measure, recognise and reward in-role CEOs for successfully stepping up?

Figure 10: Questions for Execute

Execute

Own your own development – here are some critical questions you should ask yourself to get started and to reinforce your actions

Plan

- Have I translated my strategy into a simple, easy to communicate and execute plan (for myself and others)?
- Is every stakeholder involved clear about the plan and their role in it?
- Have I anticipated where problems / challenges could arise and have I got a contingency plan?

Manage

- What managerial skills do I need to develop to best help me to manage both tasks and people / stakeholders?
- How do I manage things when its going well and how do I manage challenge and tough conversations?
- What do I expect from my manager in terms of on-the-job support and coaching?

Solution orientation

- How knowledgeable am I about problem solving technique and execution?
- When the going gets tough or we come across roadblocks how do I encourage others to find solutions not problems?
- How do I keep a positive, solution mindset when the pressure is on?

Figure 11: Questions for Excel

Excel

Own your own development – here are some critical questions you should ask yourself to get started and to reinforce your actions

My development

- Am I clear about my own strengths, gaps and action steps? (eg 4Es assessment)
- Have I completed my first 90-day plan?
- Do I have a robust personal development plan, supported by my line manager?

My support

- How do I interact with individuals who are part of the implementation team?
- What relationship / rules of the road do I need in place with my line manager?
- Who would I value ongoing feedback from to help me develop my skillsets?

My team

- How do I build and develop high performing project / task teams?
- How do I engage other stakeholders who may not be part of the organisation (partners, customers, independent workers)?
- How do I map and manage my key stakeholders from start to finish?

This 36-question coaching guide will help support the personal development journey involved in unleashing the inner CEO, as an important accompaniment to the formal online assessment and interactive coaching conversations between individuals, line managers and other stakeholders in that journey. This ensures that all candidates are supported, in the right way, to develop the knowledge, skills and behaviours essential for success as an in-role CEO and beyond.

The outcome of the assessment and question toolkit informs what training and coaching may be needed. It will also become clear who the best person is to sit with to learn from as candidates develop the required knowledge and skills.

The 90-Day Road Map

Designed to be modified to suit the various organisational and personal needs, the road map is a model incorporating the main activities and expected output. You can also download a visual of the 90-Day Road Map from *The Inner CEO* webpage.[47]

Figure 12: The 90-Day Road Map weeks 1-12

Modify to Suit Your Organisation and In-Role CEO Profile

Week	Main activities	Output
1	Establish parameters within which to operate. Role clarity. 90-day goal and road map, including project focus, additional activities beyond job role and learning plan (mosaic menu). Establish senior leader as sponsor and informal mentor outside line management support. 4Es self-assessment and resulting development plan.	A mutually understood and agreed plan which can be shared across the business.
2	Initial learning activities. The 4Es understanding and skills build (training and on-the-job coaching) . Develop ideas for special projects and new ideas.	Understanding skills gaps and strengths, understanding and business case for up to 2-3 new ideas and projects for in-role CEO to lead.
3	Initial learning activities. The 4Es understanding and skills build (training and on-the-job coaching). Activate new project or focus area for in-role CEO to lead.	Agree initial in-role CEO focus areas or project. Kick-off and key measures or milestones agreement.
4	Project team kick-off and robust project actions. Agree mobile digital tool to drive communication and collaboration efficiencies (reduce email!) eg Trello, Chanty, Slack, WhatsApp; also to help track project progress and exchanges (Trello). Possible project management training if available (or personally secured learning around project management principles and use of tech such as Trello).	Mobilise, engage and communicate with stakeholder groups and update on objectives, measures, roles and responsibilities. Establish communications parameters and rules.

Week	Main activities	Output
5	Month 1 review – learning, action, roadblocks, successes and requirements for continued progress. Analysis of any impact on job-role focus and discussion – 4Es assessment review and personal development plan modification. Ongoing project action and communication.	Management and HR awareness of progress, successes, gaps and support requirements. Ongoing ownership of new projects and developments.
6	Possible secondment or co-working with mentor, key managers or leaders in the business as sharing of best practice and ongoing personal development for in-role CEO.\n\nOngoing project action and communication.	An introduction to the wider business and how some key leaders and managers operate to ensure best practices and add to own personal in-role CEO toolkit.
7	Month 2 learning activity (formal training or on-the-job coaching sessions) – personal development mosaic actions driven by in-role CEO in parallel with company activity. Ongoing project action and communication.	Implement modified learning plan following previous week and refocus personal development on must-have leader and manager skill sets to support ongoing project management.
8	End of Month 2 stakeholder and project team reviews (progress so far on actions and initiatives etc). Formalised feedback loop from stakeholders – temperature check re knowledge, skills behaviours.	Feedback useful to modify personal development plan and ongoing learning and project or stakeholder focus.

Week	Main activities	Output
9	Ongoing project action and communication. New learning plan initiated with on-the-job support.	Full focus on job role and special project or initiative.
10	Ongoing project action and communication. New learning plan initiated with on-the-job support.	Full focus on job role and special project or initiative.
11	Project progress measurement and consolidation with team and manager in advance of week 12 senior leader review, including next steps and new ideas generation.	Opportunity for formalised line manager review and consolidation of learning, results, needs and ideas; feeding into presentation to the senior management the following week.
12	Presentation to CEO or senior leader sponsor of objectives, actions, results and impact on business and people, plus next actions, new ideas and ongoing road map planning.	Consolidation of first 90 days' actions and initiation of forward plan for action and learning and support.

As you'll see, Week 1 of the 90-Day Road Map covers the operational parameters, role clarity and the 90-day goal, including the project focus. It also includes additional activities beyond the job role and learning plan.

The output of the first week must be mutually understood and the plan agreed, before sharing it across the business. Based on what's been agreed in Week 1, a training course may already be organised, with candidates pre-booked, so they know exactly what's coming up. It's about job coaching and developing ideas for special projects, independently and with the line manager.

This is exciting because this is where unleashing the inner CEO comes alive. It's where workers begin to have more autonomy and a say in what they're going to be working on over the next 90 days.

They start by owning their 90-day plan and the development path that goes with it. The outputs are based on a deep understanding of skill gaps and strengths.

It could be that each person enrolled in the 90-Day Road Map is encouraged to come up with a maximum of three new ideas or projects. Achieving significant progress with more than three may prove difficult, if individuals and their line managers become overwhelmed with too many new projects in addition to their usual role. It's essential to unleash inner CEOs systematically, rather than rush in without adequate preparation. It is, as you can see, very much a step-by-step process.

Weeks 1–4

The initial stage of Weeks 1–3 is about learning activities and ensuring a skill build on the job. This is where a sound grasp of the 4Es model, with an assessment and development focus, is essential. It's then about moving towards the activation of one of the new projects, or development of one of the new ideas generated. The output is agreed.

In Week 4, it's project kick-off stage, where it's essential to make sure that key measures and milestones are agreed and in place. Let's say a new project has been identified. Robust project actions are required, and it's also a great idea to agree which mobile digital tools will be used to drive efficient communication and collaboration. The goal is to reduce time wasted going back and forth in the old, less productive way of working.

Tools such as Zoom, MS Teams, Google Workspace, Slack and Workplace by Facebook are worth exploring further to connect, drive collaboration, encourage open and secure communication and more. They are great for in-role work, project work, small collaborative groups, events management and much more. Also, where more formalised projects and tasks need to be managed, with multiple strands running in parallel, I recommend tools such as Trello and Notion. Of course, there are also more specialised platforms such as Asana®, Microsoft Project™ and Smartsheet® to consider.

In summary, the outputs for Weeks 1–4 are:

- Agree the outcomes for the first 90-day plan

- Mobilise, engage, communicate with stakeholder groups

- Update on objectives, measures, roles, responsibilities

- Establish communications parameters and rules for the ongoing project

This completes the first month of the 90-Day Road Map.

Weeks 5–8

Week 5 is the perfect time to review learning, actions, roadblocks, successes and what's needed for continued progress. It is an early opportunity to sit down with the line manager, project team and peer coaches to assess progress so far and identify what feedback has been received, what is working, what needs tweaking and what further support is required.

It's essential to include an analysis of any impact on the job role, as we've covered before, because you've got to make sure that the day-to-day job performance is being met, not just the new projects. At this point, it may be necessary to have a more robust discussion about the outputs of the 4Es assessment and to modify the personal development plan to make sure required learning is supported. It's now possible to see the reality of what's needed as opposed to just the planning theory.

Week 5 outputs are management and HR awareness of progress, successes, gaps and support requirements and ownership. This is where we see the concept of ownership coming into play as people develop their projects.

Week 6 brings us to the halfway mark and is about co-working and adopting best practices. Here we also consider what makes a great leader and a great manager, and what happens in other departments, so that candidates begin to get a much broader view of what's going on throughout the company, not only in their team.

Week 7 is a good spot for additional formal training and on-the-job coaching sessions to keep the momentum going. At this point, we're aiming for the personal development actions from the Mosaic menu (in the following section) to be driven by the individual, in parallel with company activity and ongoing projects. The week 7 output is the implementation of the modified learning plan.

Week 8 is about stakeholder and project team reviews. This is the first opportunity for formal reviews. There must be a formalised feedback loop for stakeholders, and temperature checks around knowledge, skills and behaviours so that you can gauge what's working and what's not. This requires the in-role CEO to be thinking about what needs modifying as part of the personal development plan. This includes the organisation of ongoing personalised learning and day-to-day coaching.

The outputs for Weeks 5–8 are:

- Management and HR awareness of progress, successes, gaps and support requirements

- Ownership of actions, embedding and sharing new practices
- Implementation of the modified learning plan
- Stakeholder and project team feedback

Weeks 9–12

Weeks 9 and 10 are about getting on with the projects and tasks. It's the combination of doing and learning as the central themes of the 90-Day Road Map. During Week 11, it's important to consider the effectiveness of all the activities in play, start to measure project or task impact and consolidate progress with stakeholders in preparation for a senior leader review in Week 12.

This should be a high-stakes meeting at the end of the 90 days at which candidates are required to deliver an impactful presentation to the CEO or another senior leader. Therefore, the required output of Week 11 is the opportunity for a review and consolidation of results, learning and ideas. This review should be with the line manager and the project stakeholders at all levels, and should feed into the senior management presentation planning, preparation and practice in advance of the final week.

The focus of Week 12 is the delivery of the final presentation, which talks about objectives, actions taken, results secured and the impact on the business and people throughout the 90 days. The output focus isn't the presentation, but the preparation required to consolidate the results from the 90 days. This then leads into creating a new 90-Day Road Map with next actions, new ideas, appropriate training, coaching and support.

It's designed to be a stretch, but it's undertaken in a safe environment when you use this comprehensive toolkit and put the necessary systems in place. It's an opportunity to fast-track learning and become a leader, no matter what your official role or level is.

The outputs for Weeks 9–12 are:

- Measurement of project or task impact and consolidation of progress with stakeholders
- Review and consolidation of results, learning and ideas
- Delivery of presentation for review at senior leadership meeting
- Creation of your next 90-day plan

There's also a Personal Development Mosaic in the in-role CEO's toolkit, which covers 15 categories of things people can do for their development as they execute their 90-day plan: individually and with support at organisational level.

As you can see below, the mosaic contains a menu of options which covers *knowledge, behaviours, leadership skills and advice, management skills* and *personal skills*. This is not exhaustive but provides a starting point to find the right personalised learning blend to move forward. Each blended learning path will look different for each person and provides plenty of ideas and concrete actions to take forward. No doubt it will also spark other ideas, which of course can be included in an expanded mosaic.

Let's look at an example of how it works. The first five columns of the mosaic are addressed to in-role CEOs, so that it is ready for them to use to create their own personal development plan. Therefore, the guidance that follows the table is also addressed to them directly.

Figure 13: Personal Development Mosaic to Support the 90-Day Road Map (menu of first ideas and options)

Knowledge		
Digital learning Internal videos Self-driven learning	Time with leaders and managers to learn from them (mini interview and key success factors)	Read articles and watch self-help videos on how to lead at any level in an organisation

Behaviours		
Who models great leadership and management behaviours in your business? Highlight what you can do and practice (your perspective, your peers and from manager perspective)	Sit with HR and talent and understand how values link to organisation culture and the valued behaviours internally for the best individual contributors, managers and leaders	Feedback from manager and peers – what traits do they value you for and what would they advise you to do differently to step up?

Leadership Skills		
Secure senior level mentor and specific training, learning action as defined with HR and talent liaison	Online learning – for example: • LinkedIn Learning, Tigerhall app • strategic thinking • leadership versus management principles	Take the lead in projects with close support, feedback and coaching from your line manager or other manager – specifically around leadership knowledge, skills and behaviours

Management Skills		
One-to-one coaching from your line manager or most suited manager On the job observation	Project and project team management training plus co-working with experienced project manager to learn the ropes and secure tips, tricks and traps	Interview a strong manager in the business for best practice advice (including HR perspective)

Personal Skills		
Interpersonal effectiveness – training provided by your company eg communication, collaboration and EQ	Emotional Intelligence assessment, learning and application	Team building, development and performance training / coaching / formal and informal feedback activity

4Es self assessment as foundation stone to identify strengths and gaps and development plan

Organisational Level Support		
Make leadership skills demonstration a part of performance measurement https://www.artsprofessional.co.uk/magazine/article/leading-all-levels	Reconnect employees to higher and wider purpose beyond job role – it's worth being and staying here https://www.artsprofessional.co.uk/magazine/article/leading-all-levels	Performance and behaviour-based recognition and reward pathway for stepping up 'in role' (avoid career blockages and reward as broader contribution in role)

Row 1: Knowledge

Digital learning is classified as the first component in the *knowledge* option. Self-driven learning could comprise watching educational videos to build your skill set, such as increasing remote working best practices, virtual collaboration and communication must-dos, and so on. You have to be prepared to step up and seek out the resources that will give you the edge.

The second component is about figuring out how you can spend time with leaders and managers so you can learn from them at first hand. The third component is reading articles and accessing developmental videos about how to lead at any level in the organisation. Some of the links at the end of this book are a good place to start.

Row 2: Behaviours

The second row then gives you options to work through around *behaviours* that you can model and cultivate, using some of the ideas included.

Row 3: Leadership skills

The third row looks specifically at *leadership skill sets* and where you can seek further advice, inputs and learning, such as having a mentor, attending training and driving your own self-development.

Row 4: Management skills

The fourth row moves from leadership (focusing on and doing the right things) to management skills: the how-to. How do we do things in the right way when working with, engaging and mobilising others?

Row 5: Personal skills

The fifth row considers the support for a personal skills suite to enhance those all-important interpersonal capabilities. These used to be called soft skills, but to me there is nothing soft about them. These are today's power skills to unlock relationships, collaboration, tough situations, team performance, networks and much more. Here we look at the personal effectiveness training to be provided by your company around interpersonal effectiveness, such as communication and collaboration, including written and verbal communication, as well as things like presenting skills.

The other essential personal skill that we know sets great leaders apart from the merely 'good', is emotional intelligence. In terms of training, an emotional intelligence assessment is key for the personal development of in-role CEOs. It could be done as part of training from a qualified line manager, or formal training undertaken by working with an emotional intelligence certified practitioner. Emotional intelligence is so important when unleashing your inner CEO that I incorporate it into the support and development programmes I design and deliver for organisations globally.

The final row then adds in the organisation's own responsibilities in supporting the in-role CEOs as they embrace their developmental journey. This, mixed with the personal ownership of their learning, provides a robust, multi-strand approach to the support and development of people who are unleashing their inner CEO and stepping up to the challenge. The Mosaic is designed for in-role CEOs to work their way through the different components and create their own personal development plan, strongly supported by the organisation.

Some of this may be a bit uncomfortable as people address where they need to improve their skills and confidence, but taking ownership of their self-development is a significant part of unleashing their inner CEO. Keep in mind that this is a menu of options. It's not essential to do all the things, but individuals can pick the ones that are relevant and right for them, based on their goals and the feedback they've received so far.

That's a summary of the Mosaic menu and the things to be looking at for your development or that of your people. The 90-Day Road Map, 36 Questions and the Personal Development Mosaic provide a powerful, practical toolkit for unleashing the inner CEO. As you can see, it is necessary for an organisation to provide support, not only through **creating the conditions** for individuals to unleash their inner CEO, but also through the **ongoing activities and personal development journey**.

In this new paradigm of the rapidly evolving future workplace, it should no longer be just about measuring the KPIs for a specific job role. Managers must learn to appreciate and recognise those stepping up and taking ownership of their development, in addition to delivering on the job.

This is about giving everyone who is ready to achieve more the freedom, encouragement and training to do so. By enrolling in the 90-Day Road Map, people are effectively raising their hands to say, "Yes, I'm ready." Suitable candidates must want to step up to the challenge. We can't force anyone to be motivated to do more, but existing leaders can make it irresistible to anyone who desires more purpose in their job and life. The vision becomes more than just one of what the company is trying to achieve from a revenue generation point of view. It becomes an inspiring vision of possibility for everyone involved. It's about being awake to the broader purpose beyond individual job roles. And as Michael Chavez and Sudanshu Palsule describe in their book, *Rehumanizing Leadership: Putting Purpose Back into Business:*

> "Purpose is the life-force that runs through us and our organizations. The words we use to describe its presence are words like direction, passion, wellbeing, productivity, clarity, engagement and even joy. Organizations with a sense of purpose that goes beyond shareholder value are more productive and innovative."[48]

How can in-role CEOs start to operate in this new way of being? How can they support others to do so? By being enabled and empowered to lead with purpose, in a way that frees up their talent to innovate and excel, rather than limiting them to what they already do. We must all be encouraged to be more conscious of the ripple effect our actions have, not only on our customers but on our colleagues and communities. It's essential to be aware of the social impact we have as an organisation, and to model the behaviours we'd like to see more of, internally and externally.

This is the future of work. And that future is now. The toolkit outlined in this chapter provides an extensive practical framework for what is needed to begin to put all these elements in place.

When people feel supported, appreciated and recognised for their contribution, not only to business health but to a higher purpose, everyone involved and connected to the company will be impacted in positive ways.

ACTION: you can access more details, toolkits and templates on my dedicated webpage at https:// performanceworks.global/theinnerceo

What Next?

In the next chapter, we'll look at how to measure employee empowerment and make sure there's a return on effort and investment. Before that, our next interviewee, global learning leader and specialist Philippe Bonnet, considers what happens when organisations unlock the power of their people and unleash in-role CEOs. Philippe passionately believes in the power of collective and collaborative leadership and how that can multiply business growth efforts.

INTERVIEW WITH
PHILIPPE BONNET

" ...the intangibles: engagement, motivation, commitment and collaborative mindset ... are so essential because if you don't measure these, the day will come when your people will stop putting in the extra effort and focus purely on their job role."

Philippe Bonnet, vice-president, global head of learning and organisational development and HR business partner, Essilor International

Philippe Bonnet lives in Singapore and the scope of his role with a worldwide company covers most global markets. He combines senior management experience in diverse, multicultural business environments with longstanding expertise in coaching at executive level. His passion lies with people and equipping teams with the knowledge, skills and behaviours needed to thrive and grow, in an increasingly uncertain workplace.

Jeremy

You have had experiences on a global scale and seen the potential of people when they are empowered. In the spirit of this book, *Unleashing the Inner CEO* within our people, what must be in place at the organisational level for this to take off and succeed?

Philippe

The first thing is the people; if you have the talent in the organisation and don't have to look elsewhere, you have the main ingredient for success. Then it becomes about the supporting structures you have in place and the executive leaders who will drive it. To get people to buy into the vision, you need to be able to sell it to them. It's like being a farm. There are so many different versions, and you have to decide what kind of farm you want to be. For example, if you're eco-friendly, you must focus on high quality and create the ability to market and sell your products.

As a company, if you talk about what you aim to become, and bring people along on that journey by mobilising them behind your purpose, you create the climate for engagement, commitment and success, which is perfect for unleashing inner CEOs.

Jeremy

What skill sets do our unleashed inner CEOs need to display to ultimately be successful in and beyond their job role?

Philippe

In terms of development and characteristics, they have to be able to deliver results, and have a command of broader business capabilities beyond their job role, as well as a series of supporting skills. Communication and the ability to influence and inspire, no matter what level they are in the company, are at the heart of it. You have to help people to grow those skills quickly as they start their leadership journey at their level, and the company must get behind them with the right training, mentoring and coaching support.

Jeremy

Why do you think it is so vital in the current climate for organisations to embrace a flatter structure and truly empower people to unleash their inner CEO?

Philippe

Simply put, it's because of the speed of the transformation we are experiencing. We need to adapt and do things differently. A traditional leader cannot adapt quickly and must mobilise the power of curated leadership. Leaders at all levels need to deliver results in their job and contribute to the health of the whole business, whether at the strategic or operational level. And this has to happen fast because speed changes a lot of things, such as how we think about our businesses, how we structure them and how we have to continually adapt.

So, leaders at all levels need the enhanced capability to foresee and anticipate actions, implications and shifts. They need a big picture view, and they also need a view from the ground. By curating our approach to leadership, it enables rapid identification of issues, opportunities and challenges at strategic and operational levels, and this way, things can happen at supersonic speed. I think it's more about the hare rather than the tortoise; it's turning traditional thinking on its head, and companies everywhere need to understand this is a question of survival, not a choice. Speed, not size, wins.

Some traditional companies have a magic formula that has carried them through for years: a magic recipe that allows them to sell something familiar and consistent across generations. The problem is they are so rigid that they forget they can still adapt, change and do things differently while maintaining their magical essence, which is who they are and what they mean to their employees and customers.

Kodak is a good example. It was all about the purity of film versus digital. If they could have embraced the new, as well as keeping the secret ingredient of the image – the captured moment, rather than the hardware – the story could have been different. All that was required was a simple shift to focus on the output and impact, rather than the raw ingredient and format.

Embracing that simple shift and including everyone in the journey is the first step to starting to create the environment and culture where curated leadership can flourish. That has to be driven by those at the top, and the trust of those executive leaders is critical for people to buy into the vision, particularly when they see them acting on their words and being role models for the way forward they are advocating.

But that trust is easy to lose if they aren't authentic, and their behaviour and modelling can make the difference between success or failure. Think about Jack Welch at General Electric; whether you are a fan or not, the guy had a positive impact on the rest of the organisation through his behaviours, passion and ability to empower others in the execution of the vision and transformations. This is evidenced trust; counter that with the ex-CEO of Nissan Japan: Carlos Ghosn. The impact of his behaviour, his actions and the actions of the broader leadership around him will have done lasting damage to everyone in the company. It will stop empowerment, risk-taking and leadership at all levels, and it will encourage more people to leave than to stay. We will see what happens, but that is my view of the situation.

Jeremy

This can positively impact how our unleashed CEOs model themselves when they look up the line and observe the behaviours and actions of their executive leaders. They have to have the right motivations, don't they?

Philippe

Our unleashed inner CEOs are people who can create their brand rather than just mirroring what they see, which is essential. Still, they need the judgment to model the best bits and to understand the potentially damaging behaviours and attributes of others. These considerations are important starting points as they help to very quickly identify who is suitable, who is less so, and where a robust development plan needs to be put in place.

We need to ensure that our people have the right motivations to step up and deliver more, supported by the company but within their evolving leadership brand. That is how I see curated leadership.

Many people are leading at all levels, in different ways, and it's the differences that have the most impact. We need different leadership styles and skill sets for various projects, situations and challenges. It's crucial that at the organisational level, we support this development with targeted, personalised learning as well as standard approaches. We need mentoring and coaching to support the process and to bring out the very best leadership traits in our unleashed inner CEOs. This is empowerment that works – without the necessary support it will evaporate and fail, creating a negative legacy.

Jeremy

From your perspective as a global learning leader, how do organisations support their people as they unleash their inner CEOs?

Philippe

This has been one of my challenges, and my conclusion is that it is about the initial assessment process, not so much from a selection point of view, but an assessment of the knowledge, skills and behaviours essential to leadership at any level. There is a starting point, a personal learning journey and then clear support from the rest of the organisation. It also helps to understand whether someone will progress into executive leadership and has the capacity and the will to contribute at their level in different ways with new projects and future expansion of the current role.

The balance is then one of how we support each person on their journey, and how to keep them developing as motivated, engaged, rewarded and committed individuals. To support this goal, I recommend that companies appoint a new kind of CEO: meaning a chief empowerment officer. If our executive leaders, including the current CEO, repurpose their role with this mindset, it builds a successful path to follow. Something for leaders at all levels to think about is not only how they step up personally but how they can empower and bring out the best in others.

Jeremy

Like me, you have lived and worked on a global scale for many years, so how does our concept of empowering others and unleashing the inner CEOs in our companies operate across borders and cultures?

Philippe

People's cultures, as well as company cultures, are significant influencers. So, for example, an international company working in Japan or Brazil that embraces the 'think global – work local' approach, and tailors it to provide the best for its employees, can get the best out of the international situation. You can create the environment where you empower them to a higher degree than a local company, typically, so it's seen as an advantage rather than a disadvantage. Taking into account the different styles of leadership and cultural approaches, you can unleash the inner CEOs globally. This personalised approach removes bias, encourages inclusion and creates a greater sense of belonging, where varied ways of operating are embraced and developed for the benefit of everyone.

For this to be effective, you also have to be able to track results from a business and a personal perspective, so I recommend also appointing a chief evaluation officer and a chief emotion officer to structure and personalise the approach on a deeper level.

Jeremy

So beyond cultural personalisation, what other things should we have in place from a developmental point of view to help unleash our inner CEOs successfully?

Philippe

Change management principles are the foundation as we look at both the 'we' and the 'I' levels. 'We' as the company and management: what do we do to communicate and support the change? And then what do 'I' do to manage my change journey, in line with the company change vision? It's a combination of collective and personal responsibility to ensure the successful change in the minds, and the modelling of empowered leadership.

Jeremy

What's the impact on the organisation, internally and externally, when we unleash the inner CEOs successfully?

Philippe

The critical impact to measure is the extra value or the additional engagement we derive from our people. It revolves around the intangibles: engagement, motivation, commitment and collaborative mindset, which are so essential because if you don't measure these, the day will come when your people will stop putting in the extra effort and focus purely on their job role. If you get the focus on the important intangibles, then the growth of the business, results and other performance measures will track upwards.

Think of impact as an iceberg; what you see are the tangible features, but what supports it is underneath. We can argue that qualitative intangibles are more relevant to measure from day one than anything else. Do it well: support and encourage the process, and the measurables will look after themselves.

The very best companies recognise these factors as central to success, and they create recognition and reward around the qualitative as much as the quantitative because they are so strongly related. Rewarding behaviours, attitude and actions beyond KPIs is a great approach, and is why many companies are turning away from traditional performance management; it doesn't account for these factors.

An excellent recent example is what happened in the PSA Group (Peugeot Group of companies). Its profitability, customer satisfaction measures and quality consistency were high, and the leader at the time recognised that this was driven as much by individual commitment and passion as it was by hitting tangible targets. He announced that as a reward for those who contributed to the results, he was going to give €4,100 to every employee who earned less than double the minimum salary. This is the part of the workforce that didn't usually receive a bonus like the rest of the organisation. A part, nonetheless, central to success, who had unleashed their inner CEO and went beyond role description and expertise, with total commitment, which is what I referred to as curated leadership. And they were rightly rewarded for it.

Jeremy

As we head into the next decade, we are seeing an increase in the independent worker population. It's likely that our workforces will become more blended; permanent staff and independent workers will work side by side, more formally. How do we empower people who may even not be permanent employees?

Philippe

I see this trend happening, and companies have to think about it. The first thing is to create a connected ecosystem for all our workforce, whether permanent, contracted, independent workers or other stakeholders. This would be an ecosystem that allows us to communicate and collaborate effectively, with appropriate technologies and management support, but enables everyone to do more, own more and contribute more, whatever their level. If we get that right, everyone – even the independent workers – will be satisfied.

Whether they are specialised or not, overall, it means that specific resources can be directly focused on tasks aligned to their specialist areas, rather than in more traditional environments where they might force-fit employees from one side of the business to another. So, we not only have specialism; we also empower them to lead and own their contribution at far higher levels to collaborate with others in a living ecosystem, designed to support the growth of our resources and business.

In the spirit of unleashing your inner CEOs, the blended workforce is more beneficial because you get ownership and expertise in one package. It's how you support, manage and continue to develop it that determines whether the resource is permanent or increasingly populated by independent workers and retained contractors.

Jeremy

So, considering our overall theme of unleashing the inner CEOs within our people at all levels: if organisations don't do it, what's the cost of maintaining the status quo?

Philippe

It's the loss of opportunity, lack of innovation and an inability to attract and retain the talent the company needs. It may still survive for a time, but it will be only through short-term focus and fighting on the frontlines, which is not sustainable for long-term business health. The companies that embrace a mentality of experimentation, and acknowledge the power within their people, will have the greatest success.

"Embracing that simple shift and including everyone in the journey is the first step to starting to create the environment and culture where curated leadership can flourish."

Philippe Bonnet

CHAPTER 6:

Measuring Employee Empowerment

Introduction

When organisations are making such a fundamental shift to encourage their brightest and best to unleash their inner CEOs, there needs, of course, to be a return on effort and investment.

It reminds me of the adage, "What gets measured gets done." When we're measuring the newly unleashed in-role CEOs, there should be a combination of two sets of components: qualitative and quantitative, both at the organisational and personal level. And when these come together, it makes it possible to assess the effects of individuals and their teams stepping up and taking ownership, and the impact it has on the business.

As we've covered, this is exciting and productive because it creates a far bigger ripple effect than job role results alone. It's also worth noting that while we must measure our unleashed inner CEOs, we must also continue to measure how boards, executive leaders and line managers are stepping up and how the culture of the organisation is adapting, to create an environment where unleashed inner CEOs at all levels thrive.

This chapter outlines detailed guidance for measuring progress at the individual level. It then provides a series of questions relevant for gathering both qualitative and quantitative data at organisational level, including a focus on employee engagement and the impact of this on external branding, as well as on turnover and internal employee satisfaction measures.

Tracking the Progress of In-Role CEOs

Once we have everything in place, balancing qualitative and quantitative measures (internally and externally), we must consider how to best track individuals' progress. Is the organisation successfully building the leadership pipeline? Are individuals and teams working efficiently and effectively? Are the right people on the journey? Once candidates are on the programme, are there clear improvements across the 4Es? On the personal side, is the feedback from the senior level and peers demonstrating an improvement and is it impacting results delivery?

These are the kinds of metrics and considerations to take into account when measuring the quantitative and qualitative components. Once you can track movement in these metrics, it also becomes easier to understand where productivity gains have been and the extent of those gains. A benefit of greater productivity is a greater organisational focus and an impact on business results, short term and in the creating of forward pipeline and growth pillars.

The organisation and the individual are responsible for taking ownership of the measurements of empowerment when unleashing inner CEOs. It is not down to the individual alone, nor to line managers. The very nature of stepping up to unleash the inner CEO means operating as a leader. Leaders take responsibility for themselves, for their team and for their results. To enable a culture of empowerment such as this, it requires a root-and-branch involvement to make sure it works for the organisation and for the in-role CEOs.

90-Day Road Map Tracker

It's critical to measure results from day one, so to help with that, I've devised a checklist to track the completion of the 90-Day Road Map activities. The 90-Day Road Map Tracker is aimed at individuals who are using the 90-Day Road Map to unleash their inner CEO. You'll see the same 12 weeks of activities as in the road map table, but this is about measuring the progress and impact. How we measure the activities comes directly from what we've already established as our road map, so this final table completes the toolkit and is simple to follow. I'll take you through an outline of the tracker.

Figure 14: 90-Day Road Map Tracker

Week 1

As you can see, Week 1 is about setting and agreeing on the parameters within which to operate. In the Measure column, you would aim to have a signed-off road map and plan, as well as senior-level alignment. The agreed training, coaching and mentor resources would be in place, and the key people at senior level would be fully briefed. The 4Es assessment would be completed as part of your first week's activities.

Week 2

For Week 2 measurements, the first training course or session is complete or under way. Candidates would be familiar with the 4Es and will have generated new projects or ideas they will be working on during their 90-day plan.

Week 3

In Week 3, the project team has been activated, and feedback gathered on the plan, which will be refined if necessary. There will have been a one-to-one with the manager mentor to go through the assessment results and to subsequently create a personal development plan, including details of relevant self-help resources.

Week 4

By the end of Week 4, the project is in progress, and you would have a collaborative communication framework supported by some kind of digital tool to manage the project, which has been set up, shared, explained and understood by all members of the team. You will have evidence of progress via formal project tracking and updates, enabled by a mobile-first tool, such as Trello, or an internal platform. A project management course has been organised, if needed.

Week 5

With your first month's review completed, both job performance and unleashed inner CEO performance have been tracked. You will have the opportunity to talk about what has been achieved, the roadblocks you have faced, and your expected performance for the next month, based on what's happened in the first month. And your plan for the next 30 days will be further refined in terms of personal development, prioritisation and expectations.

Week 6

By Week 6, formalised co-working sessions for self-development have been completed, as well as a one-to-one with the manager and mentor to debrief and feed into the ongoing development plan, which may be further tweaked after the review of actions. There has also been a review of what has been executed through your project tracking and a chance to go in a slightly different direction, to refine your approach or to choose to continue in the same way.

Week 7

This is about evidenced ownership of self-development through a completed learning log, which will be based on the Personal Development Mosaic actions and formalised company training undertaken. This is the first opportunity after seven weeks to review what you have learned and what is needed to move forward. The other measurement will be a review of project activities and milestones on the current plan.

Questions to ask at this stage include:

- Are you delivering as per expectations?
- Do you have any roadblocks?
- Is there a plan B in place?
- Do you need to discuss the plan further with a line manager to create a road map of corrective action?
- Is there interim communication with the project team as you approach another completed month?
- Is there clarity of direction, and are there progress issues, solutions and actions going forward along with any amendments you're making to the project, to the timeline or the team?

Week 8

By the end of this week, a full review has been completed, and the plan for the next 30 days be agreed. Tracking of both job and unleashed inner CEO performance is required.

Questions to ask at this stage are:

- Are you still achieving what you need to within your job role, as you follow the plan to unleash your inner CEO?
- How is your project progressing in terms of deliverables, collaboration with others and clarity of communication, both vertically and horizontally?
- Do you have clarity about what you need to achieve in the next 30 days?

This is an excellent opportunity, after eight weeks, for an informal feedback loop around knowledge, skills, behaviours, progress, unleashed strengths and gaps from not only your line manager but also your project team.

Week 9

The measurement here is about the answers to the key questions and actions you implemented following the Week 8 review. It's an overall temperature check, covering personal development, progress updates and mutual feedback to note what's going well and what pressure points are emerging. The temperature check can also relate to the qualitative emotional factor, covered previously, in addition to tangible goals achieved.

Across Week 9 and Week 10 is a focus on project deliverables and ensuring that you are on top of your specific job role must-dos is imperative.

Week 10

This is about continuing project and team management which may require another one-to-one session to review results, progress and objectives. This could be supplemented through informal feedback discussions with members of the project team and other stakeholders to gather further directional advice and personal development tweaks. Week 10 is similar to the previous week, so the primary measure of success is the same.

Week 11

This week requires a formal project review with the manager and mentor, a look at the results so far, a consideration of informal and formal feedback from others and, finally, the planning for the presentation to the CEO in the final week. This can include role-playing, one-to-one coaching support and other forms of practice to ensure a high degree of personal readiness.

Week 12

The final week will be measured by the delivery of the presentation to the CEO or other senior-level person and the consideration of actual qualitative and quantitative results set in Week 1 and refined throughout the 90-day cycle where relevant. Formal feedback from seniors, peers and the project team will then be discussed with your manager and mentor. The next 90-day plan will be agreed with supporting learning and development in place.

An agreement for the next 4Es progress assessments will be completed, which I recommend should happen in the range of six to nine months following the initial assessment. The goal is to have achieved an ongoing, measured discussion throughout the 12-week process. The business will know the qualitative and quantitative impacts of what's happening at an organisational and at a personal level. There should be no surprises for anyone involved because open discussions, adjustments and tracking have been constant since Week 1.

This completes the current cycle of the 90-day plan and is a perfect time for a period of reflection, not just for those who have been unleashing their inner CEO, but for all leaders and managers involved. The 90-day plan culminates in the completion of a big commitment as well as a significant measurement, so it's an opportunity to take a breath and review what's been achieved at the personal and the organisational levels.

Making it Personal: The Six Centres of Me

There's an emotional or personal side to the qualitative element of unleashing the inner CEO. Whereas the quantitative aspects can be measured primarily through the 90-Day Road Map and impact on the business, the qualitative elements are more personal. It was necessary to create a model to measure this, called The Six Centres of Me. It's about going beyond results to get a real sense of immersion in this new way of operating. It's about understanding how it impacts the individual and in turn the impact on others, the business and the working environment.

The model is made up of six topics on which to reflect so that you can measure the success of the personal side of unleashing your inner CEO. The questions themselves can be owned and considered by each in-role CEO and then be part of a coaching conversation with their line manager or other stakeholders.

Figure 15: The Six Centres of Me

My Centre of Autonomy

My first centre is autonomy. Do I feel a degree of independence, empowerment and freedom from constraints to unleash my inner CEO in my job role and beyond?

My Centre of Self-Motivation

My second centre is self-motivation. Am I energised and able to achieve my personal vision with commitment and enthusiasm, without feeling pressure from others?

My Centre of Self-Confidence

My third centre is having the belief in my capability, energy and skills for success as an unleashed CEO.

My Centre of Self-Efficacy

My fourth centre is self-efficacy. Do I have the ability to control and deliver desired results for me, the team and the organisation?

My Centre of Job Satisfaction

My fifth centre is job satisfaction. Do I feel appropriately recognised and rewarded for my contribution above and beyond my specific job role?

My Centre of Relationships

My sixth centre is about relationships. Are my relationships meaningful, collaborative and productive? Am I able to bring others along with me at all levels as I contribute beyond my specific job role?

This is a temperature check from an emotional standpoint, which we don't often talk about or we don't talk about enough. We know we're heading in the right direction because there are things we can do at the quantitative level, which relate very clearly to the organisational activities and to actions in the 90-Day Road Map. The quantitative component is critical for success, alongside the qualitative elements such as The Six Centres of Me.

Furthermore, The Six Centres of Me is a tangible model for people to take ownership of and to measure their experience, which is a more complex thing to do. This is the all-important emotional side to their personal development, of which we must be aware. Of course, for this to really come alive, involving the line manager, HR and other stakeholders in the conversation will help to establish the facts as well as the feelings and identify progress, while leading to more obvious, supported, personal development action.

The Culture of Autonomy

In an interesting article, 'Empower Employees to Make Things Happen',[49] Marina Krakowski examines the business transition towards a culture of autonomy. The article covers how organisations have traditionally operated in a culture of compliance but need to transition to a culture of autonomy for a more productive workplace. This is at the heart of the shift I'm proposing as organisations create in-role CEOs.

A culture of compliance encourages bureaucracy in organisations and is characterised by habits such as managers avoiding risk and decision-making. Conversely, a culture of autonomy focuses on the right things to do and moves towards how to service customers and employees better. Managers coach their teams, rather than merely assigning them tasks.

As a result, employee engagement is higher, and staff turnover is lower. Decision-making should be occurring at every level of the organisation, and this is precisely what we're aiming for when unleashing inner CEOs.

Krakowski writes about a fascinating example of the culture of autonomy:

> Joanne McInnerney, SHRM-SCP, witnessed this as vice president of human resources at Novelis, an Atlanta-based maker of rolled aluminium with about 11,000 employees worldwide. Under previous management, a top-down decision-making approach gave front-line employees the impression that they didn't have the authority to make decisions or even voice concerns. After a new CEO set more customer-centric goals for the company, empowerment began spreading as a natural consequence, she says. Once employees knew what the goal of 'delighting customers' looks like, they began to speak up when an order wasn't meeting specs. The old focus on maximising shipment volume and revenue had, by contrast, prompted employees to allow defective shipments to go out despite their better judgment.

> "We all want to be part of something bigger than ourselves," said McInnerney, "so if you feel able to speak up and are given control, you're going to automatically like coming to work."

It's natural for us all to want to be part of something bigger than ourselves. And if everybody has permission to speak up, we can do things more efficiently so that levels of customer satisfaction increase. And then in turn, when employees feel appreciated and that they're doing something worthwhile, their satisfaction automatically increases too.

Freelance journalist Zara Stone wrote an article for American Express, which further reinforces how empowering employees boosts business ROI.[50]

"Human capital is 2.33 times as important as physical capital," she wrote, referencing research by Angela Carter, senior client partner at Korn Ferry, on the impact of employee empowerment.

In this research, Carter wrote, "It's a CEO's most valuable asset for improving performance, mitigating risk, delivering productivity and future success. The benefits are twofold. The ROI on employee empowerment is good… It increases productivity, and they'll stay loyal to the company or loyal to the brand even if they move on."

Zara Stone concluded that treating employees with more attention is a great benefit to companies.

Considering Both Qualitative and Quantitative Measures at Organisation Level

"Research indicates that workers have three prime needs: interesting work, recognition for doing a good job and being let in on things that are going on in the company."

Zig Ziglar

When we're looking at an empowered organisation, which is essentially what unleashing inner CEOs at every level creates, there's going to be a significant impact on the company.

Let's look at the first set of components as they relate to the organisational level. The qualitative element would show up in everyday work as individuals demonstrating a can-do attitude, and it would be easy to spot positive changes in their behaviour, by asking these questions:

- What evidence is there that the 90-Day Road Map is driving a positive mindset *within* the company as a whole?

- How are the developments impacting organisational culture and levels of employee engagement?

- To what extent is increased collaboration and communication happening?

- Where across the organisation are you able to notice emerging leadership management traits? What attitudinal changes are you noticing; for example, do employees seem content when you interact with them? Do they seem more resilient in the face of challenges?

- Are we building the culture of autonomy we promised, rather than just talking about it?

When taking on new projects and operating with greater autonomy, it will be necessary for in-role CEOs to handle situations and pressures that they may not have had to deal with in the old hierarchy. As we covered in the toolkit, being solution-oriented is paramount.

In terms of the organisation's duty of care as you empower people to unleash their inner CEO, I like the quote from Ian Hutchinson, author of *People Glue*, "Your number one customers are your people. Look after employees first and then customers last."[51]

I appreciate this perspective because it's keeping in mind that there are people in the organisation who we need to accompany on the journey, because they're going to need support. And when we support and recognise them, we have the opportunity to help them excel in the long term, not just for short-term gains. In summary, the qualitative element measures are what we're looking for in a person's development. They become the glue to attract high performance, strong contribution and growth.

Once we have embraced the importance of managing qualitative measures, we can also consider the quantifiable efforts to prove impact on core internal measures and external business growth.

A few considerations might be:

- To what extent is employee satisfaction increasing?

- What impact are we starting to evidence through our customers, partners and other stakeholders externally?

- What specific benefits are our customers experiencing?

- How are customer satisfaction measures being impacted? Are customers noticing a difference?

- Is our business growing?

- Can we separate our organic growth curve and incremental revenue gains through unleashing our inner CEOs?

- What is the impact on our overall bottom line and functional KPIs?

- How are the developments put in place to unleash inner CEOs impacting attraction, recruitment and retention of our workforce?

- How are our employer branding measures being impacted?

It will be important to embed ways of asking these questions throughout the organisation: for example, as part of regular consultations with everyone, at all levels. This way, examples of success as well as patches of slower implementation may be identified and explored.

Putting Our People First

"To win in the marketplace, you must first win in the workplace." This is a great quote from Doug Conant, ex-CEO of Campbell Soup Company. In order to realise the results we are targeting, we've got to focus internally in creating the foundation and climate for in-role CEOs to thrive. This requires work, at all levels, on mindset, culture, workplace practices and workforce effectiveness, because these are the things that will impact the quantitative measurements at organisational level.

This includes, for example, internal engagement measures, employee satisfaction improvement and the organisation's overall employer branding performance externally, as much as internally. Not only will this contribute to business growth, but it will also help assess how much more attractive the organisation is to those seeking employment. Particularly those who want to be part of something exciting and empowering, whether they are looking for a permanent position, or are a part of the growing independent workforce engaged by companies globally.

This is a relatively new battleground from a marketing, recruitment and retention perspective. Organisations must find ways to measure whether employees feel more connected to the company and explore how to increase connection. Potential employers must become more appealing as people appraise them externally and decide whether they'd like to work for them. To attract loyal employees and top talent, be it permanent or independent resource, organisations need to ensure that potential recruits can see things clearly when reviewing their employment options.

For example:

- Does the company have a great way of working?

- Does it have a great structure in place?

- How high is employee turnover? Is it reducing?

It's worth bearing in mind that potential employees can frequently see online reviews, so it's essential to manage the company's reputation, not only for customers but across the board.

Final Word

Leigh Branham and Mark Hirschfeld wrote, "It's sad, really, how a negative workplace can impact our lives and the way we feel about ourselves… most people go to work at jobs they dislike, supervised by people who don't care about them, and directed by senior leaders who are often clueless about where to take the company." [52]

This reiterates my earlier points about how many companies are not ready for the new era and the true age of empowered employees. You cannot unleash in-role CEOs with a culture such as this, as the initiative will be doomed to fail. A period of reflection must also be embraced by senior leaders and line managers as they come to terms with a different way of working and how their working focus and impact on the business has changed since unleashing our inner CEOs.

To wrap up this chapter on a more positive note, I love this quote from Steve Jobs, "The only way to do great work is to love what you do." As you can see, what executive leaders do to help themselves and their employees to love the organisation, love what they do, love the sense of empowerment and love being at work is so important for creating truly empowered, motivated and high-performing in-role CEOs. It's at the heart of the 'spirit' of what we are trying to achieve and is so important for the emotional component of the journey, not just the business road map.

What Next?

In the final chapter, we'll look at the bigger picture of what I've shared throughout this book, and the incredible opportunity we now have to reimagine our organisations amid continuing global uncertainty, disruption and an increasingly distributed workforce, and also opportunity.

First, the interview with Andrea Studlik points to how the upsurge in remote working has accelerated digital enablement and must be supported by flatter structures of coaching, collaboration and communication. Andrea discusses how establishing a safe environment is the responsibility of everyone in the organisation, and how a robust infrastructure needs to support this.

INTERVIEW WITH
ANDREA STUDLIK

"We all have a responsibility in creating a culture whereby mutual help, peer, project team coaching and collaboration become the key ingredients to success."

Andrea Studlik,
senior director of talent management, Asia Pacific,
Jones Lang LaSalle (JLL)

Andrea Studlik is a senior level, global human capital expert, with working experience across borders and cultures. Andrea is currently senior director of talent management, Asia Pacific at JLL, and before that, was director of learning and development and campus head at AXA University, Asia.

Jeremy

What does leading at all levels mean and why is it important in the 2020 workplace?

Andrea

It's about the collaborative nature of work. All the stuff I'm working on now is project-based. Even though we have annual plans and it's the same year-on-year, we work in multiple teams across multiple geographies and we're all peers, but you've got six or seven people. None of us are bosses of others and we have to manage ourselves.

We have to manage our deliverables, our priorities and our stakeholders, once we get off the phone with each other. So, collaboration is more and more a critical skill that we need to be teaching for how to manage and lead projects in this way to develop.

Jeremy

That's a good point. And I suppose in the new flatter organisations, you have to take ownership. So, thinking about individual contributors who perhaps don't have that much experience in order to know what to do, we have to also think about how to train them and model behaviours. It's increasingly important they step up, isn't it?

Andrea

You just reminded me of something. There was a project where we had more junior employees on the calls because they were the ones doing the work after we agreed the strategy. Our expectation was that they would complete the tasks and deliver on schedule. So, they had to take ownership and there was a need for lateral thinking. We work for a global company, on global projects, and we all see the same problem through different lenses. These guys need to be able to anticipate the expectations and requirements, dependent on what's happening, not only with people in their own office but also in various time zones and cultures and so on. That's hard to do. It does take a different skill set to be able to implement.

And the thing that you reminded me of is that we, as the more senior people, have a responsibility, which even I didn't realise until just now, and that is to help those who are stepping up on those weekly calls to clarify goals, stay on track, create open feedback loops, have informal coaching moments and help them prioritise, so they have a fighting chance of being successful and flourishing.

Therefore, we all have a responsibility in creating a culture whereby mutual help, peer and project team coaching and collaboration become the key ingredients for success. For everyone.

Jeremy

Is this a natural evolution of where organisations are going now, or is this a call for a revolution in how we work, collaborate and unleash the inner CEOs of individual contributors throughout organisations?

Andrea

It has been largely evolutionary but perhaps some may need a mini-revolution to accelerate it and formalise it. It's more important than ever to help people discover meaningful work, empowering them to unleash their inner CEO. If we consider the situation right now, of those of us working from home, many are having trouble motivating themselves. They need to feel more connected to the work they are doing and to the people they are working with.

So bold new rules of the road, collaborative ways of working and a more robust support infrastructure are needed in many organisations. Remote working is developing new muscles to flex in all of us, and they need to be trained and toned up.

As I do more and more of this myself, I'm also realising just how important regular communication, coaching and support through managers are, in enabling and accelerating this evolution of working practices.

Jeremy

Interesting. So, if you consider how this is evolving in your current business, has this been a cultural shift within the company?

Andrea

The thing is that we haven't been building or focused on culture. We have to define it first. It's just starting now. We're still working on a values campaign to focus on skilled leadership. So, it's never been something created, it just is new. You feel it. We are fortunate that the natural culture of this company is already collaborative, welcoming and supportive. A great foundation for how we now build on that.

Jeremy

So, for any organisation that does this well, they look at the change required, with the right leaders in place and then identify people who can step up at all levels, empowering them to a far greater degree. As a result, they're contributing beyond their job role, perhaps to something more strategic. What's the benefit to the company and the people?

Andrea

For the people, it's definitely accelerating their development. Maybe it's one-sided of me to think that it's because of the growth in project-based work, because all over, even at my previous company, everything was a project. There were a million and one project names, you know, like Project Sunrise, Project Sunset and so on. Everybody was working on one or more projects and that's what makes it come to life. They're managed by multiple people. It's not that you just have your line manager, you're responsible to many people.

Everybody has to own it. You have to keep yourself accountable to your own part of the project and how you can support others.

Jeremy

So, as all this comes together, what is the role of the line manager?

Andrea

To me it's very much like the saying, "It takes a village to raise a child." In the workplace, it takes this community to support one other, and a line manager to consolidate, provide clarity and make things come to life. I would argue that in new, flattened, more empowering structures it is the community that trumps the line manager in supporting, peer coaching and developing those unleashed inner CEOs across our businesses at all levels.

For example, I interact with some of my colleagues' team members more than they do with their line managers, because they're supporting me and doing what I need done. So, my feedback about their contribution, challenges, development areas etc is required. I coach them informally. It really works. It's so cool.

Jeremy

What's in place for those individuals who step up and unleash their inner CEO? What tools do they have at their disposal so that they can do some self-development?

Andrea

Well, this is where it's a bit loose in each region. This is one of the things being worked on. The Americas region is probably the most far ahead with the development that it offers and not necessarily the quality, in my opinion, but the number of development opportunities that they have at their disposal. It's not just training programmes. They've got conferences, they've got job share opportunities. They've got secondment opportunities. We are formalising this across the other regions to support everyone who needs it. It's a key factor for successful empowerment across the company.

Jeremy

So, it's important to give everyone the right tools and support they need.

Andrea

Yes, it is. But the legacy challenge is that we have too much traditional learning delivery (face to face etc). This is good, but we can make this more efficient with greater digitalisation and mobile-based learning.

We are working on this but from my experience many companies are still locked into how they used to train and develop people, using old playbooks, traditional approaches and not changing the game around *what* needs to be developed, and how to best deliver the training, coaching and personal development.

Jeremy

Some traditional leaders may still believe they have all the answers and enjoy the hierarchical way of doing things. What do you say to those who are resisting unleashing the inner CEOs within their people?

Andrea

I think it's a really limiting belief, and maybe it's generational, maybe it's cultural, I don't know. These leaders may have a reinforcing internal dialogue, "In order for me to look good, I have to have a bunch of junior and less talented people below me." And that's completely the opposite of what's true. When I think about all the greatest leaders I've known, it's because they showed vulnerability and they showed, "I've got an amazing team who are better than me... I had to go get somebody better than me because I don't know everything." And that makes them stronger.

Jeremy

Oh, it does. And then you are truly unleashing the power of the people, aren't you?

Andrea

Exactly, because if that person has the confidence and the strength to just sit in that and admit that and be OK with that, it starts to make it OK for others to show that vulnerability as well because it's safe to do so. I think that here in JLL, what makes the difference is that our CEO in this region is like that. It's infectious and entirely positive.

A key success factor is how he holds his executive team accountable. He puts two things together: the ability to be vulnerable and to expect, "I need more, I need better than me," and at the same time, holding people accountable in a respectful way. It is a very strong trait, and with such a trait, leaders, in my experience, can create anything.

Jeremy

So, while I could talk to you all day about unleashing our inner CEOs, if there were key things that are enablers in organisations to unlock potential and give people permission to step up, let them experiment and contribute in new, value-adding ways, what might they be?

Andrea

I think the first thing that comes to mind is confidence: self-confidence. When a person is self-confident then you can let go a little bit. You don't need to micromanage; you don't have to constantly be worried whether this person is doing that thing. Are they doing this? Are they doing that? So being grounded in self-confidence. Let things evolve. Choose the best, make sure they're clear on what they need to do and then let them get on with it. I think that that ability to just sit in that knowing that, "I chose the best, I gave them what they needed. I need to let them do what they do." Giving them space is a really important thing, but you also have to hold them accountable. It's like being a good parent. I just keep coming back to that.

And as I think about where we're heading in three and five years from now, the digital side of things, and this working from anywhere at any time with anyone; there's trust. You have to trust that it's going to happen. And again, it goes back to believing that you chose the right people, you gave them the right tools and the right vision, and now you let them do it. It's this digital enablement that's really important. When I think about what I want to be doing in the next few years, I want to make sure that there are more companies that are thinking laterally or thinking without borders, that, for example, are hiring more independent workers on a much more frequent basis. We all know a lot more people want to be working like this rather than working as an employee.

"When I think about all the greatest leaders I've known, it's because they showed vulnerability and they showed, 'I've got an amazing team who are better than me... I had to go get somebody better than me because I don't know everything.' And that makes them stronger."

Andrea Studlik

CHAPTER 7:

The Opportunity to Reimagine Our Organisations

Following the Covid-19 pandemic, we had to create the 'next normal'. Before that, business transformation was important, but now it's become critical.

For years I've been researching and saying that business transformation consists of two components: the *human* and the *digital*. As we've covered in different ways throughout this book, *human* is the workforce and methods of working, and *digital* is the technology component that enables the human component and the organisation as a whole to function.

Before the 2020 pandemic, over 80% of organisations failed in their digital transformation initiatives. Too many focused primarily on the technology and systems and ignored the human component, which is evolving with the rise of the gig economy; with increasing numbers of independent, flexible and remote workers; and many more complexities of the digital revolution.[53]

The pandemic was a catalyst which accelerated digital transformation because if companies wanted to trade, in most cases they had no choice but to embrace the digital. In January 2020, before the Covid-19 outbreak was declared a pandemic, 44% of companies in the world did not allow remote working, whereas just 12 weeks later, over 80% had integrated remote working into their business model, with most beginning to explore how remote working could continue.[54]

Megatrends have also been spotlighted because of Covid-19. Positive impacts on short-term climate measures highlighted what is possible if we live and work differently. Consumerism was refocused on the must-haves, not the nice-to-haves, and exposed the big global issues we still have to deal with, in parallel with our business and workplace transformation.

There is still a reliance on fossil fuels and mass consumer-based capitalism, as well as other trends such as inequality, climate change, diversity, and sustainability. All of these raise many questions and pose numerous problems for businesses to address in their continuing operational, digital and human transformation. Will the next normal for business regress to 'how things were', largely ignoring these global macro factors? Or will we and our businesses reimagine how we can go forward in a more diligent, considered way to balance the needs of employees, customers and consumers with the needs of the planet?

These are big questions for our subject matter, and something we all have a duty of care to think about and do something about. Perhaps with leaders at all levels, comprising a diverse mix of people, a variety of generations and broader viewpoints, we have the ingredients for positive action, rather than just talking about it. We will see. That said, there is clearly an excellent opportunity to reimagine business, rather than getting back to how we've always done it.

A helpful question would be, "What if we tried something new?" This is the best chance companies will have to implement what we're talking about in this book, and also impact the bigger ticket, macro items such as digital transformation, the future workforce and more – in other words, the five forces outlined in Chapter 1. Because of unavoidable circumstances, they've already had to begin transforming. They must seek the next normal to survive and thrive beyond the 2020s.

There has never been a better time to unleash inner CEOs throughout organisations and involve them in flattening structures and redesigning business. Let's start with meaning and purpose in a brave new world where we empower people rather than attempt to rebuild broken, obsolete systems. This way, the executive leaders will be free to focus on megatrends and strategy, while the rest of the organisation takes care of the execution, led by their growth mindset. Too many senior leaders will miss this opportunity because they will be preoccupied with survival, instead of building the company for future success.

Even companies that weren't thinking about more radical transformation now have the opportunity to leapfrog the traditional journey and start with a blank piece of paper to envision their future organisation.

Some savvy companies have announced that they won't go back to how things were. PricewaterhouseCoopers, Twitter, McKinsey and

Barclays, to name a few, said during the Covid-19 pandemic that they have found new and better ways of working. Some have discovered that more empowered staff are focused on the must-dos, and this is helping reduce the 'white noise' that can add unnecessary work and burden on to managers and individual contributors. They are rapidly adopting new ways of working and discovering, often with some surprise, that they are more productive, efficient and effective internally as well as in how they work with customers and external stakeholders. They're joining remote working pioneer companies whose workforce already comprises 50% remote workers, such as Google and future-ready companies like WordPress, which already works 100% remotely.

My previous prediction based on my research of the blended workforce (that is, independent workers, permanent workers, remote workers, new ways of working and new places of work) was that more distributed and self-driven working would be commonplace by 2025. I have since re-evaluated the data in the context of the 2020 pandemic and predict that the five-year journey to transformation will be condensed into two years.

During this transition, the need for leaders at all levels who are autonomous, engaged, motivated, supported to unleash their inner CEO, thereby contributing in and outside their job role, is even greater. This drives the flatter organisational structure we have been talking about throughout the book and provides a new framework for managing a more diverse workforce, which will increasingly be made up of independent workers and contractors, working alongside permanent employees.

Part of this develops the ideas from Petra Kuenkel's book, *The Art of Leading Collectively: Co-Creating a Sustainable, Socially Just Future.* A more collective approach to leadership can be the secret to sustained, shared success and mutualised growth.[55] I have built on this to propose that 'collective and collaborative leadership' brings two elements into play, gluing together collective leadership and the mindset of collaborating to grow. Like many things we have proposed in this book, it starts with mindset and then shifts into implementing and operating as 'the way we do things around here'.

Figure 16: Collective and Collaborative Leadership Model

The concepts, ideas and proposed actions in this book are designed to help organisations build their own version of collective and collaborative leadership by unleashing the inner CEOs within their teams. The interviews throughout this book are designed to serve as a barometer to measure progress: they are a temperature check for companies to assess their roadblocks, their opportunities, their starting points, and the milestones on their journey to enabling successful collective and collaborative leadership at all levels. The interviewees have done this and are still doing it. Their commentary supports the ideas in this book and provides a glimpse of what could happen when you do it. You will discover best practices, traps to avoid and watch-outs to have in mind. You will be able to fast-track your own next practices, as you encourage your organisation to unleash its inner CEOs.

We're able to pinpoint which organisations are in the driving seat and progressing more rapidly than others. These organisations are geared to unleashing their leaders at all levels in the business, regardless of where those inner CEOs are based, their level, their gender, or their employment status. Incorporating this awareness into our thinking is a great way to embrace and confront big-ticket challenges for businesses such as diversity, equity and inclusion issues, because unleashing our inner CEO helps to transcend the old mindset. It is by nature inclusive, collective and collaborative. We must naturally embrace, include, and drive a sense of belonging throughout modern organisations. To maximise progress, we have to be more tolerant of different ways of working, whether those who work with us and for us are permanent employees, part-time workers, remote operators, independent workers or partners.

What this means is that by creating an organisation fuelled by unleashed inner CEOs, we have a unique opportunity to reimagine the business and how it works, internally and externally. This thinking accelerated through the Covid-19 pandemic, as organisations were forced into the transformation and into pioneering new ways of working. It unlocked the desired mindset, which is a perfect foundation for organisations everywhere to unleash leadership at all levels.

We're talking about getting into a 21st century mindset and leaving the 20th century legacy behind as we move forward.

We also have to understand how to leverage our entire network and build engagement, motivation, success and growth for everybody involved. And a truly enabling and empowering atmosphere will do that, making sure that the right technologies are in place to allow everybody to work and contribute. Clear guidance with rules of the road and support infrastructure, which we have covered throughout this book, need to be in place first. The onus is on the organisation, and then it's down to the management and the individuals to embrace it. We need to create inclusive environments, removing the diversity and bias lenses that have been blockers in many traditional workplaces. Something we need to focus more on is diversity of thinking. This is the mindset that unlocks possibility, creativity and experimentation, and sets the in-role CEOs free.

Empowerment, ownership of ideas, creativity and innovation come from our leaders at all levels, which allows us to build a more resilient business model from the ground up. We have experienced a pandemic, and we're also going through the VUCA world: volatile, uncertain, complex and ambiguous. I have evolved VUCA to **VUCAD:** my 'D' is for 'distributed', as we move into new ways of working, doing business and operating remotely. This isn't just an experiment and forced-to-do any more, but the next normal. It will continue to challenge many organisations and individuals.

Figure 17: VUCAD

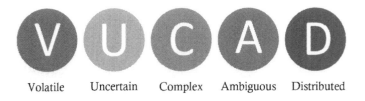

On top of everything else, we also know that we've got another transformation coming as we head towards Industry 5.0, the Fifth

Industrial Revolution, heralding the autonomous era: next-stage technologies; people supported by more intelligent, integrated and adaptable AI; robotics; personal support automata and fuelled by megadata, which makes our VUCAD world appear somewhat more 'manageable'.

By building a more resilient business model now, we'll create a structure which more easily adapts for the future; it means that organisations won't have to transform all over again, completely. We will be ready to adapt and evolve rather than undergo another revolution like the one we're experiencing now.

The results of implementing the material in this book will underpin the rapid organisational transformations we have witnessed in recent times. A more collective and collaborative mindset in leadership terms means that you will have empowered, unleashed in-role CEOs on the ground, delivering beyond their job description. This also results in executive boards and senior leaders having the time to focus on the megatrends and the big growth strategies driving what the organisation delivers to employees, customers, shareholders and other stakeholders in the medium and long term. Organisations will be ready to adapt to sudden changes, big technological leaps and the continuing integration of digital into how we live, play, work and do business.

These 'new' boards and executive leaders will need to select close advisers, including non-executive directors (NEDs) and strategic consultants, with care.

In fact, one of the core purposes of NEDs is to contribute towards strategy, based on their broad and varied experience. However, NEDs who have enjoyed careers in traditional offices and have managed teams face to face, in an office environment, may struggle to contribute to future strategy if they lack digital transformation and virtual working experience. This will particularly be the case if they have not sought to mobilise, engage, empower and support people who are dotted across the map, enabled by appropriate and productivity-centred technologies. That leaves big questions for many organisations to ask themselves at the senior-most level:

- How virtual-savvy is our executive board?

- How digitally mature are we as a board and how does that translate into reimagined strategy definition and execution?

- How do we adapt our organisational culture for an increasingly remote and blended workforce?

- How does this shape our strategy at organisational and management level?

- What new pillars do we need to build in support of emerging ways of working?

- How do we move from bricks-and-mortar to more distributed ways of operating?

- How comfortable are we with a flatter structure and a more empowered workforce?

- What new learning and development do we need at executive board level to help us better navigate the future?

- Who are the new breed of NEDs and advisers who can better support our business over the next decade?

- What do our customers expect of us now and over the next decade?

It will be imperative that any adviser to a business with a flatter structure, driving leadership at all levels, rapidly adopting digital and embracing new ways of distributed working, is experienced in working in this new environment. They need to have a proven track record advising leaders in the new corporate era, rather than relying on traditional, 20th century legacy thinking and ways of operating. They will need to advise very specifically on governance evolution and the financial underpinning of this brave new way of working; they will need a location-free mentality to unlock borderless talent integration, service offerings and operations. This would include the possible moving away from permanent offices to remote hubs and homeworking, as well as building the new organisational culture, new go-to-market modelling and a more data-driven, agile approach to strategy, decision-making and rapid implementation.

This raises the question of readiness for some existing NEDs, executive board members, senior leaders and the business as a whole. Are they ready to adapt? Are they ready to adopt new models, new ways of working and more? Or are they still locked into 20th century thinking and slowing down the transformation of the organisation they are supposed to be leading or advising? Rapid evolution is driving more empowerment through organisations. Why? Because it cannot happen without everyone contributing to the whole, as much as within their job role: it's more of a collective and collaborative mindset, supported by committed executive leaders, who take hold of the strategic navigation of the organisation, focusing on the big picture (again).

Those making a lot of false starts and those who are sticking with traditional leadership approaches – micromanaging their employees, practising command and control, rather than a mindset and approach to unleash and empower people – are slow to transform. This simply has to change. Therefore, 'readiness' at executive leader, NED, strategic adviser and management level is key to unlocking a new age of empowerment in organisations, as well as unleashing the inner CEOs across businesses and embracing leadership at all levels. If the executive team members are not ready, are slow to act or are just starting their own transformational journey, this will impact the level of true empowerment that will be granted.

Figure 18: Speed of Transformation and Relative Level of Empowered People

	SLOW ← Speed of business transformation → **FAST** (Digital and Human)
HIGH	• Generates excitement and creates wider pool to support and contribute to the transformation agenda • Inclusive and diverse culture • Keeps people motivated and interested • We together versus us-and-them • Watch out: old thinking versus new ways of working could cause tension • Short to medium term only before people may get impatient with pace of transformation • Emerging politics / cliques – the rapid movers and the slow movers	• The pace of change requires leaders at all levels who are capable of contributing in current role and strategic direction • Inclusive, diverse culture with strong sense of belonging • Collaborative, clarity on direction, flatter structures to unleash inner CEOs • Culture appropriate for the new era • New thinking and new ways of working – agile, forward-looking company and people • Attractive company (employer branding) • Better retention of talent
LOW	• 20th century thinking versus 21st century thinking • Culture and politics need to change • Strategic and operational tension • Leadership immobilisation possible • People feel constrained • Fear of speaking out • Cookie cutter versus cookie palette	• Controlling leadership not willing to risk losing power • Hierarchical nature persists • Transformation could falter without buy in of management and people (particularly if not empowered or engaged in the journey) • Short-term focus makes company myopic, missing greater opportunity • People and talent are not part of the process or engaged • Attraction and retention issues into the medium term

Level of empowerment (vertical axis: LOW to HIGH)

Speed of business transformation (Digital and Human) — SLOW to FAST

As you can see in Figure 18, I have provided an indicative four-box model for your business, function or leadership team, which can be applied broadly. The focus is on what is happening at an organisation level and combines the speed of transformation with levels of empowerment. This model is to help you to understand the current situation, mapped against where you need to be, as well as to help you to define a considered route map to attain your goals.

As an example, considering this model, if your speed of transformation is slow, and your level of empowerment low, then you have a 20th century thinking business, not a 21st century one. This creates strategic and operational tension, and people typically feel constrained, versus when you're fast and moving at a highly empowered pace, which creates an inclusive and diverse environment in leadership terms. This pace of change naturally requires leaders at all levels and is collaborative, with a culture appropriate for the new era.

As another example, if you are slow but driving high levels of empowerment, there is a balance of short-term excitement, mixed with medium to long-term frustration, as transformation does not keep pace with in-role CEOs who wish to push boundaries and speed up change. This could lead to increased politics, old-style management reappearing and, worse, talent being disillusioned and leaving the company, which makes it all the more difficult to attract the right kind of replacement. A negative cycle is hard to break when your people, who are being empowered, are thinking in 21st century terms, while the organisation is stuck in the 20th century and making slow progress.

In the interviews, our experts reinforce and demonstrate the in-role CEO model in a multitude of different roles, industries, backgrounds and cultures. They have one thing in common: they all support and encourage unleashing the inner CEOs within our organisations, to make leadership at all levels a reality. They see this as the next important and urgent step in corporate evolution and have been championing the cause in their own ways. In-role CEOs help executive leaders to focus on the megatrends and build new ecosystems whereby people can more easily contribute, solutions are more tailored, networks are more collective, and everyone takes ownership and is accountable.

Many of the interviewee experts observed that horizontal power is vital, and the vertical, hierarchical way of doing things is no longer helpful (while acknowledging that there still needs to be some form of hierarchy in place to lead and manage the new era). They reinforced the need for flatter structures so that leaders can navigate the choppy waters of the future, help unleash inner CEOs, and execute and protect the short and medium term. Perhaps it's not quite the full holacracy I mentioned earlier, but it's certainly a more collective and collaborative approach to the leadership of our organisations.

The other commonality that stood out in the interviews was that organisations can embrace a diversity of skill sets, trumping the old style of power or skills kept by the few. In the recent past, it was common to have special projects, populated with the chosen few. The same environment reserved expert training, coaching and 'talent tracks' for selected individuals. This, by very definition, was exclusive, not inclusive.

If we are to unleash our inner CEOs, we must think more inclusively. With more diverse skill sets developing in more people, there's a better opportunity to reinvent the business within the more resilient, future-geared framework we've discussed. It's an exciting time because when we have more leaders at all levels in the organisation who are knowledgeable, skilled, and who are modelling the desired behaviours, it means we can truly unleash the power of our people, supported by the modern structures, processes, training and coaching that needs to be in place.

This challenges human capital and human resources leaders to step up and support this bold, human transformation to create unleashed, empowered, motivated and valued in-role CEOs across our population, whether permanent employees or valued independent and contractor resource.

To conclude, I'll summarise the key messages from the interviews, which emerged as critical factors for success in a new manifesto for successful leadership at all levels.

Figure 19: A Manifesto for Successful Leadership at All Levels

In-role CEO success factors according to our experts:

1 A new, empowering leadership mindset at board and executive leadership level.

2 A culture underpinned by behaviours and values that are consistent with the desire to unleash leadership at all levels and empower employees to new heights.

3 A can-do mindset throughout the organisation to embrace and own leadership at all levels, beyond job roles.

4 A reimagined, flatter organisational structure that removes layers of management.

5 Repurposed line management support underpinned by a growth mindset, driving a strong coaching-led approach in support of their unleashed CEOs.

6 A climate that supports experimentation, learning from failure and rapid adoption of next practices.

7 A bold learning and development support plan to provide the strategic and operational knowledge, skills and behaviours required for leaders at all levels.

8 A platform of psychological safety promoted by human capital and human resource leaders to enable everyone to have the courage to step up, to make mistakes without being judged, to be supported and to feel safe to challenge the status quo with open debate and feedback.

Ultimately, all of this will allow unleashed in-role CEOs to grow as highly contributing leaders at all levels. This in turn supports their own leadership journey as they contribute more broadly, rise through the business and develop their own career path.

Everyone needs to be accountable and responsible for growth, theirs and the organisation's. Engaged, mobilised and motivated people are central to creating this ideal environment, which links to satisfaction in a job role, and also attracts talent into the business and helps to retain people. Attraction and retention naturally take care of themselves, whether with a permanent workforce or an increasingly loyal independent workforce of people who want to work for you and with you.

What Next?

In this book, I have provided the framework for your initial assessment of the business and your people, your 90-Day Road Map to get started, and the learning and development plans to support your execution steps.

It's time to unleash the inner CEO!

How to Get Further Support, Training and Guidance to Unleash Your Inner CEOs

I have a series of supportive keynote presentations and consulting, training and coaching solutions, available globally, for organisations that are ready to accept the challenge of becoming a 21st century business, unleashing their inner CEOs and embracing a new collective and collaborative approach to the leadership of their business.

These include:

- keynote sessions to introduce the concept to your wider audience
- leadership briefings for boards, executive and non-executive directors and leaders
- organisational briefing sessions
- the provision of a brand new human capital framework to support the implementation
- training sessions for managers
- developmental support for those in-role CEOs stepping out beyond their day-to-day job and demonstrating leadership at their level.

All my consulting, briefings, coaching and training materials are designed to unleash the inner CEOs within our organisations, to help grow their knowledge, skills and behaviours for ultimate business success. They can be delivered virtually or face to face, supported by a global network of experts who are supporting me in this endeavour. We are ready to support YOU!

Find out more about our programmes at:
https://performanceworks.global/theinnerceo

ENDNOTES

1   https://www.youtube.com/watch?reload=9&v=WdYtoj4KSeU

2   https://www.cnet.com/news/google-quantum-supremacy-only-first-taste-of-computing-revolution/

3   Katwala, Amit (November2018) *Why China's perfectly placed to be quantum computing's superpower.* https://www.wired.co.uk/article/quantum-computing-china-us

4   Micro-combs https://www.nature.com/articles/s41467-020-16265-x

5   Jeremy Blain and Robin Speculand (2019) *Transforming Your Company into a Digital-Driven Business.* Research report into the state of digital transformation. https://www.performanceworks.global/our-ideas/ticking-clock-guys/

6   Ibid.

7   https://www.forbes.com/sites/brucerogers/2016/01/07/why-84-of-companies-fail-at-digital-transformation/?sh=72ee27be397b

8   https://www.forbes.com/sites/brucerogers/2016/01/07/why-84-of-companies-fail-at-digital-transformation/?sh=4316eb29397b

9   http://www.implementation-hub.com/resources/implementation-surveys

10 https://www.mckinsey.com/business-functions/mckinsey-digital/our-insights/the-digital-reinvention-of-an-asian-bank#

11 https://www.linkedin.com/in/drrochellehaynes/

12 https://www.performanceworks.global/the-gig-hr-experts/

13 https://fortune.com/2020/05/18/women-ceos-
   fortune-500-2020/

14 https://www.theguardian.com/business/2020/jul/28/
   bame-representation-uk-top-jobs-colour-of-power-survey

15 https://issuu.com/revistabibliodiversidad/docs/dialogue_
   q2_2020_full_book

16 https://www.researchgate.net/publication/335655301_The_
   advantages_and_challenges_of_neurodiversity_employment_
   in_organizations

17 https://hbr.org/2017/05/neurodiversity-as-a-competitive-
   advantage

18 http://blonk.co/why-blonk-wants-to-be-the-tinder-of-the-
   recruiting-industry/

19 https://www.shl.com/en/blog/culture-fit-or-culture-add/

20 https://yourflock.co.uk

21 https://www.businessinsider.com/best-jobs-future-growth-
   2019-3?r=US&IR=T

22 https://www.ft.com/content/520cb6f6-2958-11e9-a5ab-
   ff8ef2b976c7

23 https://conversableeconomist.blogspot.com/2019/03/the-
   story-of-william-lee-and-his.html

24 https://theatlas.com/charts/rkJp1alb

25 https://www.goodreads.com/quotes/721301-fear-is-a-
   reaction-courage-is-a-decision

26 https://blog.jostle.me/blog/why-collaboration-is-important

27 Phygital definition https://bit.ly/30dZROt

28 https://www.goodreads.com/quotes/1198680-any-
   company-designed-for-success-in-the-20th-century-is

29 https://www.forbes.com/sites/
forbestechcouncil/2019/03/01/tech-experts-predict-13-jobs-
that-will-be-automated-by-2030/?sh=548351ad22bf

30 https://www.range.co/blog/introduction-to-psychological-
safety

31 William Craig (February 2018), 'What Businesses Need in
Order to Develop a Flat Structure of Leadership', *Forbes*.
https://bit.ly/2TVZLbs

32 https://blog.smarp.com/empowerment-in-the-workplace-
enable-your-employees

33 https://bit.ly/2TPBxPN

34 https://www.personneltoday.com/hr/crucial-create-leaders-
levels/

35 https://thriveglobal.com/stories/five-tips-to-empower-
leaders-at-all-levels-of-your-organisation/

36 https://workplaceinsight.net/study-confirms-effect-
workplace-autonomy-wellbeing-job-satisfaction

37 https://www.greatplacetowork.com/resources/blog/getting-
managers-out-of-the-way

38 https://www.forwardfocusinc.com/consciously-
communicate/empowering-employees/

39 http://theconversation.com/the-appeal-of-the-flat-
organisation-why-some-firms-are-getting-rid-of-middle-
managers-88942

40 https://www.objectstyle.com/hr/flat-organizational-
structure-in-it-companies

41 https://blog.talaera.com/2017/07/19/companies-empower-
engage-employees

42 https://hbr.org/2018/03/when-empowering-employees-
works-and-when-it-doesnt

43 https://asq.org/quality-resources/employee-empowerment

44 https://www.forbes.com/sites/strategyand/2019/02/19/
    leaders-can-cultivate-true-employee-
    empowerment/?sh=4a656ca63ab1

45 https://blog.smarp.com/empowerment-in-the-workplace-
    enable-your-employees

46 https://performanceworks.global/theinnerceo

47 Ibid.

48 Chavez, Michael and Palsule, Sudanshu (2020). *Rehumanizing
    Leadership. Putting Purpose Back into Business.* Lid Publishing:
    London. https://rehumanizingleadership.com/

49 https://www.shrm.org/hr-today/news/all-things-work/
    pages/empower-employees-to-make-things-happen.aspx

50 https://www.americanexpress.com/en-us/business/trends-
    and-insights/articles/empowering-employees-can-help-
    boost-business-roi/

51 Hutchinson, Ian (2009) *People Glue: Employee Engagement and
    Retention Solutions that Stick.* Warriewood: Australia

52 Branham, Leigh and Hirschfield, Mark (2010) *Re-Engage:
    How America's Best Places to Work Inspire Extra Effort in
    Extraordinary Times* http://www.amazon.com/Re-Engage-
    Americas-Places-Inspire-Extraordinary/dp/0071703101

53 https://www.performanceworks.global/our-ideas/ticking-
    clock-guys/

54 https://www.smallbizgenius.net/by-the-numbers/remote-
    work-statistics/#gref

55 https://petrakuenkel.com/article/collective-leadership/

ABOUT THE AUTHOR

Jeremy Blain is an award-winning international business leader, human capital expert and non-executive director. He is also an experienced executive board director in the UK and Asia (Singapore and Hong Kong). He is currently the chief executive of PerformanceWorks International, a company that helps organisations, leaders and teams succeed in the digital climate amidst disruption, opportunity and uncertainty.

Jeremy has extensive experience as a transformation leader and board-level adviser globally. He has operated in most major international markets in the world to launch successful businesses and to turn underperformance into excellence.

His track record is proven at all stages of the business lifecycle, from startup to internationalisation, raising profiles and profits throughout. On the back of this, Jeremy received International GameChanger™ awards in the ACQ5 Global Awards for two consecutive years, in 2019 and 2020.

"Jeremy has long been well ahead of the curve in transforming businesses to be led by everyone, not just its leaders, and if ever there was a time to accelerate that process, it is now."

Paul Hargreaves, CEO, Cotswold Fayre, UK; author of *Forces for Good: Creating a better world through purpose-driven businesses*

Through his business, PerformanceWorks International, Jeremy helps boards and leaders define strategies to implement digital and workforce transformations, utilising unique co-created models such as the Ticking Clock© and the GigHR© framework.

As a result, he and his team engage leaders and managers at a strategic level to develop tailored plans that drive culture change at operational level, to embed the required skills for successful modernisation. He has always been a strong believer in empowering others to achieve great things, regardless of their level. His journey as a business leader putting this into action has led to the publication of his first book, *The Inner CEO: Unleashing Leaders at All Levels*.

Jeremy has over 30 years of commercial experience at organisations including Procter & Gamble, PepsiCo, Cegos Group and in his own business, PerformanceWorks International. His varied, global experiences have led to his primary focus today in helping organisations, leaders and managers ready themselves for the challenges ahead, in the face of unprecedented workplace change and competition.

Over the past 10 years, Jeremy has also completed extensive research into digital and workforce transformation, publishing more than 30 industry white papers and research articles, as well as contributing to articles in *Forbes, CEO Today, Business Matters, Human Resources Online* (Asia Pacific), *Dialogue* (by Duke Corporate Education) and more.

He frequently speaks at international conferences and is a media commentator on topics related to the future of work, business transformation, leadership readiness, the evolution of selling and sales management, and how learning solutions need to adapt in the upskilling of human capital at all levels, in an increasingly challenging, digitally enabled and distributed workplace.

Jeremy is a guest lecturer at the University of the West of England's Bristol Business School, supporting the human resource management (international) students through modules including the digitalisation of human resources, global leadership challenges and more.

Jeremy holds a BA (Hons) from Sheffield University and Master of Management (MMgt, International Business) from The Australian Institute of Business (AIB).